STARTING OVER

HART'S RIDGE

KAY BRATT

BOOKS BY KAY BRATT

Hart's Ridge Series:
Hart's Ridge
Lucy in the Sky
In My Life
Borrowed Time
Instant Karma
Nobody Told Me
Hello Goodbye
Starting Over
Blackbird

By The Sea trilogy:
True to Me
No Place Too Far
Into the Blue

The Scavenger's Daughters series:
The Scavenger's Daughters
Tangled Vines
Bitter Winds
Red Skies
The Palest Ink

Memoirs:
Silent Tears: A Journey of Hope in a Chinese Orphanage
All My Dogs Go to Heaven

Standalone Books:
Dancing with the Sun
Wish Me Home
Chasing China: A Daughter's Quest for Truth
A Thread Unbroken
Wish You Were Here
Wishful Thinking
Caroline, Adrift

Willow duology:
Somewhere Beautiful
Where I Belong

Sworn Sisters duology:
A Welcome Misfortune
To Move the World

Children's Books:
Mei Li & the Wise Laoshi
Eyes Like Mine

STARTING OVER

A Hart's Ridge Novel

Copyright © 2023 by Kay Bratt

All rights reserved. This book or any portion thereof may not be reproduced or used in any manner whatsoever without the express written permission of the publisher except for the use of brief quotations in a book review.

Printed in the United States of America

First Printing, 2023

Red Thread Publishing Group

Hartwell, GA 30643

www.kaybratt.com

Cover Design by Elizabeth Mackey Graphic Design

RED THREAD
PUBLISHING GROUP

This book is a fictional dramatization that includes one incident inspired by a real event. Facts to support that incident were drawn from a variety of sources, including published materials and interviews, then altered to fit into the fictional story. Otherwise, this book contains fictionalized scenes, composite and representative characters and dialogue, and time compression, all modified for dramatic and narrative purposes. The views and opinions expressed in the book are those of the fictional characters only and do not necessarily reflect or represent the views and opinions held by individuals on which any of the characters are based.

PROLOGUE

*L*ydia carefully scanned each item from her shopping cart, then bagged it. When she got to the giant bag of Doritos, she was quick so that others around her wouldn't see and judge her for buying junk food when she so obviously didn't need more calories to huddle up and pitch tents around her middle. She kept scanning, meticulous with the process. The last thing she wanted was to find herself in handcuffs; it would be a crisis, especially considering she was the wife of a local deputy. She could just see Caleb showing up to the store security room and the look he'd give her when she told him she'd accidentally missed something and hadn't meant to steal it. Not that he wasn't used to the routine.

Since Walmart had mostly done away with cashiers in favor of self-checkout, the number of people, especially senior citizens, who thought they'd scanned something but had only heard the beep from a register near theirs, was growing each day. Caleb said every time he had to go make a report, he usually let them off with a warning after seeing the confusion in their eyes.

Store policy was ridiculous, and Lydia felt like their new

attempts to be more functional were making Hart's Ridge lose its small-town feeling.

But ... not her monkeys and not her circus.

She had her own group at home to tame and they always had her jumping. She looked at her watch. Hopefully Zoey was down for the night.

When she scanned the last item and the total popped up onto the screen, she winced. It was this time of year that she wondered if leaving her career to be a stay-at-home mom might've been a mistake. They could have so much more if she was still working, but then she would be too tired to enjoy her growing family. Her girls would come home to an empty house after school. And the baby would have to be with another woman all day, bonding with someone other than Lydia.

Nope. She'd made the right choice.

Her daughters were her whole world.

She paid with her credit card and pushed the shopping cart out to the parking lot.

Being a mom was the most important role she'd ever played, even if she did sometimes miss being a part of the professional world, and even her clients. She'd loved being a psychotherapist because the human mind was something that had always captivated her. One day she'd return and maybe start her own practice once she got to the empty nest part of life.

She was also a people person, as Caleb always liked to remind her when it was her turn to do the grocery shopping. And God forbid he ever take control of or even a part in planning the holidays or determining their budget and the best gifts they could get for their money.

Walmart was her first stop. She'd mostly only found gifts for Zoey, the baby, other than a few hair and makeup items for Grace and Ella. They'd want things ordered online or from the mall in Jasper, as though a bigger price or fancy name brand would make them better items. She didn't hold it against them, that was just the way of teenagers.

At least with the few items, plus the ribbons and rolls of wrapping paper she'd bought, she'd made a start in her Christmas shopping. It wasn't yet Thanksgiving, so she felt good about it, though with three daughters and two sets of grandparents, she had a long way to go.

In the parking lot, a sense of unease settled within her. She hadn't expected to be gone so long and she hoped it wasn't a mother's instinct telling her to hurry. She rarely left the baby with the girls for long, but she'd been sleeping and Grace, her eldest daughter, promised her it would be fine, to go enjoy herself.

It wasn't often that Lydia did that. Not alone, anyway.

Sometimes she had all three girls. And other times, just the baby.

Rarely ever did she have time to herself since Zoey was born.

But she didn't mind.

Most of the time.

Her steps quickened as she loaded the purchases into her car, not missing a beat. Once the items were secured, she dutifully returned her cart to the corral, came back and got into the car, and was about to shut the car door when a hand abruptly stopped it, pulling it open wide. Lydia looked up to see a man lowering himself into her car. She tried to fight him off, pushing at him, kicking wildly.

Unsuccessful, she lunged to her right, only to feel even more terrified as she saw a man standing outside her passenger side door.

"What's going on? Who are you people?" Lydia stammered, her voice trembling with fear.

"We'll explain everything soon enough," Guy Number Two replied cryptically. "Do what you're told and, I swear, we won't hurt you. Make a fuss and you're as good as dead."

Lydia felt a cold sweat forming on her brow as the men took over her vehicle and drove away from the store. The clock on the dashboard read 4:03 p.m., and her mind raced with terrifying possibilities. She wondered if she could quietly slide out her phone and dial dispatch at the department. Dottie would find her if she could just connect.

Desperation gnawed at her as they reached an ATM. The men instructed her to withdraw money, but the machine only spat out five one-hundred-dollar bills. She handed it over, and when it wouldn't allow her to take more they were furious, their anger simmering just beneath the surface.

"I can get more money, just let me go," Lydia pleaded, tears welling up in her eyes.

She tried to bargain, to reason with them, but her words seemed to fall on deaf ears.

"You're older than I thought when I first saw you, but I think we can make do with it," one of the men, Barnes, said, then leered at her with unsettling intent, sending shivers down her spine.

As they pulled out of the bank parking lot, Lydia prayed that having a cop for a husband might finally prove to be in her benefit. She studied their faces, memorizing every feature to her memory, planning for when she could see them all behind bars.

CHAPTER 1

Cate sat in her favorite armchair by the window, bathing in the warm afternoon sunlight that shone through her tall windows. Her once pale complexion had regained some color, and her eyes, though tired, held a glimmer of the fighter within. Brandy lay at her feet, Cate's constant companion and guardian, moving when she moved and seeming to never sleep as she watched over her mistress with a loyalty second to none.

Officially, Cate had rescued Brandy from an abusive owner, but Brandy had rescued her from loneliness. Brandy used to be called Moxie. A Wire-haired Pointing Griffon—a breed that was bred for hunting—she didn't have a predatory bone in her body. What she did have, along with her perfect chocolate nose, was the deepest brown eyes Cate had ever seen. She might be a dog, but she'd forever be Cate's best friend.

Taylor and Ellis were talking, going over the latest in news, what politician was cheating who, and other ridiculous political drama that November always brought. Cate had never cared about that sort of stuff. To her, it didn't seem to matter which party won the elections; after it was all said and done, whoever took the positions always disappointed their constituents. She thought you'd have to be crazy to want to be an elected official because, even if you were a saint, something would be dug up or fictionalized about you just as soon as you entered the public arena. It would drag your friends and family into it, and whoever you'd ever had anything to do with during your lifetime.

Who wanted to live like that?

She stayed out of it all and just worried about keeping her own nose clean and trying to make up her past to her family. Speaking of—with three adults and a dog hanging out in her living room—it was tight, and Cate hoped that soon she'd have some quiet time to herself before the kids got out of school and popped in to see what was happening.

Cate had never realized—when her tiny cabin was being built—that it would one day become her rehabilitation sanctuary. There hadn't been room for her cabin at the lakefront, and, though she would've loved overlooking the water, she still had a wonderful place to recover. Her home was cradled in a bend of woods, with a view of the shadowed Blue Ridge Mountains in the distance. It was therapeutic.

Cate adjusted the tube at her nose. She was still on oxygen a few times a day but, thank God, the ventilator was a distant memory.

Her journey had been arduous, filled with ups and downs, but she had fought with everything she had and now, two months after that fateful night, she was finally back home, surrounded by her family.

So far, the road to recovery had been challenging, to say the least.

After the surgery, she'd faced complications, including a collapsed lung. Later, a stubborn infection had landed in her chest and had threatened to undo all the progress she had made. On top of the physical fight, her mental state had taken a huge hit, pulling her back down into depths of dismal blackness that she hadn't felt since her first years of being separated from her lost son, and her still living daughters. The black cloud threatened to take her from the girls again, but Cate had clawed out of the deep pit with everything she had in her.

She refused to leave them again.

"Mom, you're looking stronger every day," Taylor said, her voice filled with pride as she slid the blood pressure cuff on Cate's arm.

Every one of her daughters now knew how to take vitals and analyze them.

Cate couldn't wait until she could kick the machine out of her house. She managed a weak smile. "That's because I've got the best support team anyone could ask for."

"It's also because you've been putting in the work, Cate. Don't forget to give yourself credit," Ellis said. He stood over them, watching Taylor as she pumped the cuff, then wrote down the stats on the iPad he'd furnished them. He was keeping up with all her follow-up care. Not officially, but he'd insisted he wanted to supervise what was being done to give her the best chance at a full recovery that she could possibly have. They hadn't addressed his absence from her life, and she still felt hurt. Therefore, things between them remained distant.

"Thanks. But that's because I want to get back to my life as soon as I can," she said.

Ellis was right, though. Physical therapy was a double-edged sword. On one hand, she hated it with every fiber of her being. At first, it wasn't as bad. They'd focused on gentle movements and breathing exercises to help strengthen her chest muscles and improve her lung function. With her collapsed lung, it took a lot of work to get it functioning halfway properly again.

Her small home had been transformed. What was once a nearly barren space now had medical equipment and supplies scattered throughout, evidence of the ongoing care she required. But the most significant change was her once lonely cabin now had the constant presence of her family, at least one of them always, and sometimes too many of them. Cate wasn't used to being the center of attention, and, in addition to the days that she felt so grateful to be alive and have her daughters and grandchildren around, there were also times she wished to be alone. For so many years she'd had no one, other than a good friend or two, and now her life was full.

"You know your PT is going to get a lot harder," Ellis said, his tone gentle. "When addressing muscular and nerve damage, they'll want to push you as far as they can. For your benefit, of course."

She nodded. "Yep. Dr. Reynolds talked to me yesterday and I'm ready for it."

And she was. The other edge of the sword was that the better she did in physical therapy the closer she was moving toward total independence again. They'd already started to introduce more difficult exercises to improve her strength and mobility.

Her emotional recovery was going to take a lot longer. Cate remembered every tiny detail of being shot. First, it felt like she'd been kicked in the chest by the biggest horse in the universe. She'd immediately tasted gun powder. Then everything went black. The girls said she'd still been conscious, but she didn't remember anything after hitting the floor, until she woke up after surgery.

As for why she'd stepped in the line of the bullet meant for Jackson, she really didn't know. Of course, he was now under the impression that she still loved him deeply. A part of her would always care about the Jackson she'd met as a young woman. The one who stole her away from her boring life, made her laugh, and danced with her under the stars. But that Jackson was gone just a couple of years into their marriage. The man she cared about now was simply the father of her children. As far as she could analyze, and she'd spent a lot of time doing that during the last few months, was that her girls had been through enough and, even though they all held some trauma because of the way their dad made them struggle through their childhoods, they still loved him. They'd lost enough in their lifetimes, and she hadn't wanted them to lose him, too.

The bullet was still inside her, lodged into a self-made cave in her shoulder, but too close to a bundle of important nerves for the surgeon to try to remove. Cate didn't mind. She was choosing to think of it as a badge of courage. Not that she'd tell anyone that. Everyone else didn't mention it, as though talking about the very object that nearly killed her would cause it to come back to life and try again.

Her therapist had told her how lucky she was that Eldon had missed hitting her center mass and that usually that was the easiest place to hit because it was the largest target. With all the pipes and organs behind it, most died from the shot. Cate's therapist seemed to think that telling her all these things kept Cate feeling thankful, but the truth is that she was tired of thinking about it.

The door opened and Anna came though, carrying Cate's lunch.

"Here comes the Elixir Chef Maestro," Taylor said.

Cate groaned and Ellis laughed.

"Stop it, Mom," Anna said. "Don't be a baby about it."

"Yes, ma'am," Cate said, taking the tray and setting it on her lap.

Anna oversaw her diet, and every meal included a shake concocted with all sorts of things, most that Cate couldn't even pronounce or remember, and there was always a big helping of a cooked protein. Today was small potatoes and salmon.

Cate was never a fish eater before. Other than the hockey-puck fish patties they'd served in the canteen at her prison, she hadn't touched it in decades until Anna began heaping it on her to feed her back to health.

"You're doing a great job, Anna," Ellis said. "Every bit of

protein you get into her is helping repair tissue and build muscle."

"Please, Ellis, don't give her the big head," Taylor said, rolling her eyes dramatically. "She already tries to boss all of us around."

Anna pretended not to hear while she picked up discarded items from the side table next to Cate's recliner. An empty cup, a Jell-O container, and some candy wrappers.

"Thank you, Anna," Cate said softly when her daughter was near enough to hear. "I do appreciate you."

Words of affirmation were still awkward in their family, though they were getting better about it. Even so, Taylor changed the subject.

"Saturday night. What's everyone up to?" she asked.

"Taking the kids to Cumming for ice skating," Anna said. "It was Bronwyn's turn to choose."

"That sounds fun," Cate said. "Does Teague like to skate?"

Anna shrugged. "Kind of. Depends on his mood. But Levi is going with us, so they'll be fine. Teague won't pout when his cousin is around."

"What about Jo? Is she going," Taylor asked.

Anna shook her head, looking sad. "She said she has stuff to do at home tonight. But Alice is coming."

Cate sighed heavily and put her spoon down. She didn't like it that Jo was staying home alone, once again. Since Jo's life had blown up in her face and Eldon had shown he was a psychopath who'd almost taken her family out, Jo was struggling.

"Maybe I'll ask her to come over here and sit with me," Cate said, though she had really hoped to have some alone time herself.

"She won't," Anna said. "She told me that, if anyone asks, to tell them she has plans."

They quieted until Ellis spoke. "It's going to take time, ladies. You all went through trauma, but it hit Jo deeper. She feels responsible for bringing Eldon into the circle. For having him around Levi. She knows that things could've been much worse, and she must work through that before she starts coming out of this terrible ordeal. Is she talking to someone? Professional, I mean?"

"I don't think so," Taylor said. "She's always been too stubborn to ask for help. It's why she's raised Levi alone and wouldn't even tell us who his father is."

Cate had wondered about that recently. With Jo in the emotional state she was in, it would be so nice if Levi had another parent to lean on. She'd even asked Taylor about it, but it seemed no one knew who Levi's dad was. Now surely wasn't the time to bring it up, either.

"If Jo doesn't want to come over," Ellis said, "I could go pick up a pizza or something and bring it back. If we time your medication right, we can possibly squeeze a glass of wine in somewhere."

Anna grimaced uncomfortably. "Oh, I think Dad said he's coming over later. So, he might stop in."

Cate hated the hangdog look that creeped up on Ellis' face.

"Please tell your dad I'm too tired for company later," she said. "And Ellis, I think I'm going to hit the sack early, but thank you for the offer." Her rejection wasn't to hurt him. It was to keep herself from getting any more hurt. "Taylor, what're you doing?"

Taylor smiled and her cheeks flushed quickly. "Sam's cooking for me tonight. But, on that note, I need to get to work and get my stuff done so I can get off on time."

"Be careful, honey," Cate said. "Anna, Ellis, will you walk Taylor out as you go?"

CHAPTER 2

When Taylor rounded the corner past the bank, she saw Mr. Parker in the parking lot, bent over and picking up papers he'd dropped. He wobbled precariously, and she pulled in, shut the car off, and got out.

"Mr. Parker, can I help you?" She approached, and a slip of paper caught in the wind. She stepped on it as it tumbled toward her.

He straightened, looking startled.

"I, um ... yes, thank you."

She handed him the paper and he stuffed it back into his folder. "Okay, then. Are you doing okay, Mr. Parker?"

He waved a hand haphazardly in the air. "Fine. Just fine. Gotta go."

With that he went into the bank and Taylor got back into her car.

As she drove around the parking lot, going past the drive through, one of the tellers waved frantically at her. Taylor backed up, then got into the lane and pulled up.

It was Eleanor Croft, and she put her hand over the intercom mic and leaned forward.

"Deputy Gray, I have to report something suspicious."

Taylor was suddenly on full alert, and she scanned the parking lot behind her through the rearview mirror. Were they being held up?

"What is it?"

"It's Mr. Parker. Something weird is going on with him. I think you need to investigate."

"Weird how?" Taylor asked, relieved that there wasn't something major happening.

"Well, you know how, let's say, frugal he is."

"Okay..."

"Lately he's been coming in here and getting cashier's checks. They started at around a thousand dollars and have gradually increased. I think he's sent like four now and he's back there now getting one for thirty-five hundred. It's just strange."

"Who are they made out to?" Taylor asked.

This was getting into personal information but, in a small town like theirs, they looked out for their elderly. If Eleanor Croft thought something was fishy, then she might very well be right.

Eleanor looked over her shoulder, then back to Taylor.

"Someone named Martha Bush. I don't know where she's located."

Hmm. Martha Bush didn't ring a bell. That she knew of, Mr. Parker only had a son. No daughters, and he was widowed. If he had a girlfriend, Taylor would've heard that around town, too.

"Thanks, Eleanor. I'll look into it."

"Don't tell him the information came from me," she said. "Oh, he's leaving now."

Taylor waved and pulled out, then back around to where Mr. Parker was headed to his car. She got out again.

"Taylor, what are you doing back here again?" he asked, looking nervous.

"I just wanted to talk to you a minute, Mr. Parker. Do you have time?"

He shook his head. "Not really. I must get to the post office before they close for lunch."

"It'll just take a second then. I just want to be sure that you aren't in any kind of trouble."

He squinted at her, his eyebrows coming together in one gray line.

"Trouble?"

"Yes. I mean, I don't want to get into your business, Mr. Parker, but I'm concerned. There's a lot of scams going around that take in the elderly. Some people have lost their life savings to them."

That got his attention.

He looked left, then right.

"What kind of scams?"

"Mr. Parker, this will be a lot faster if you just tell me who Martha Bush is and why you're sending her money."

He leaned in close.

"I was told not to tell anyone, but if you swear to keep a secret—"

She held two fingers up in scout's honor.

"I won a lottery," he said excitedly. "Five hundred thousand dollars."

Taylor felt her stomach sink.

"Mr. Parker. Did they tell you that you need to send them money to pay taxes and fees?"

He nodded. "Yes, but that's the way it always works. She explained it all. She's really nice. She calls me just about every day."

"Mr. Parker, I hate to tell you this, but I think you've been scammed. Let's go back into the bank and talk to them. You can at least get your money back on the check you did today, and we'll have to see about what you've already sent her."

He shook his head. "No, this is real. It's called the Dream Quest Bonanza, and I have an address in Florida to their main office."

"If it's called the Dream Quest Bonanza, why are the checks written to a Martha Bush?"

"Well, she works in their office, and she said, since I couldn't do everything on the computer, that she could help me through it. I don't like messing with that internets stuff."

"Did Martha call you today and tell you to send another check?"

"Yes, but that's because now I have to pay taxes for Florida where the lottery is, and Georgia where I'm receiving the funds."

He looked so earnest that it was breaking Taylor's heart. He leaned against his car, and she could see that his knees were shaking.

"Mr. Parker, if you win a lottery, you don't to have to pay anything to receive your winnings. They'd take the taxes and fees out of the check they give you."

"Not on this particular one. It's different because it's through the mail."

"Call her back," Taylor said.

"Call her?"

"Yes. Call her and put her on speakerphone. Tell her you have a few questions to ask her before you send the check today."

Mr. Parker hesitated for a moment, uncertainty and fear in his eyes, but then he nodded and pulled out his phone. He dialed a number and put it on speakerphone, his hand trembling as he held the phone between them.

The phone rang a few times before a woman's voice answered, "Hello?"

"Martha," Mr. Parker said, his voice shaky. "It's me, Jerry Parker. I just wanted to ask you a few things before I send the check today."

There was a pause on the other end of the line, and Taylor

could almost hear the wheels turning in Martha's mind. "Jerry, you know we don't have much time. The deadline for the taxes is approaching. That check has to be mailed today."

Mr. Parker shifted to his other foot. "I understand that, Martha, but I've been talking to Deputy Gray here, and she's concerned about the whole thing."

Taylor took the phone. "Martha, this is Deputy Taylor Gray with Hart County Sheriff's Department. I'd like to verify a few things with you, just to make sure everything is above board with this process."

There was a brief silence on the line, and then Martha responded, her voice now tinged with frustration. "Who is this? Why is a deputy involved?"

Taylor maintained her calm and authoritative tone. "I'm here to protect the interests of the citizens in our town. Now, can you tell us the name of the organization that's running this lottery, and can you provide a contact number for them? We need to just run this by the Florida Attorney General's office."

The phone clicked and Martha was gone.

Mr. Parker looked alarmed. She handed the phone back to him. "Try the number again."

When he did, an automated message came up saying the number was no longer available.

"Oh, no." Taylor sighed heavily. "How much did you send her?"

"Almost ten thousand dollars," he said, his voice trembling. "What am I going to do? That's just about all my savings. I thought I was getting five hundred thousand. I was going to surprise my son by paying off his house."

Taylor patted his arm. "Follow me to the department and Deputy Penner will help you file a report. You really are going to have to call the Florida Attorney General's office. Maybe they can help you recoup some of your money. I'm so sorry this happened to you. I wish you would've asked your son or even me, Mr. Parker, before sending someone money."

He didn't even answer, just climbed into his car and gently closed the door.

Penner took care of the cases of fraud in their county, and he was going to be angry that yet another Hart County resident was swindled.

Taylor couldn't imagine how terrible it was to lose that kind of money, and she hoped that somehow Penner would find a way to get it back for him.

AFTER A TEDIOUS BUT mild day spent processing complaints, then taking an early evening shift at the front desk for dispatch, Taylor was on her way to Sam's house and their favorite Saturday night date-night routine. A few miles out, she got a text message from Grimes, one of the other deputies.

> Call me stat, please!

She got him on the line immediately, and he sounded worried. "Taylor, I don't want to get anyone too alarmed, so I haven't called it in, but I'm getting really concerned. Lydia said she was just going to Walmart, but a few hours later she called and said she'd be gone a bit longer because she was going somewhere else. Grace told her to take her time but didn't expect it to be this long. Lydia's phone goes straight to voicemail. She's not answering my calls or texts, and that's not like her at all. She rarely leaves the baby with our teen daughters for this long."

Taylor was worried. She knew Lydia well, having met her through Grimes, of course, but they were friends. She knew Lydia as a dedicated mother, and, if Grimes was concerned about how long she'd been gone, then there was a reason. Especially the fact that she'd left the baby for a more extended time than she normally would.

"Alright, Grimes, we'll find her. Let's start by retracing her steps. I'll meet you at Walmart." She hit her brakes, then did a U-turn and headed the other way. Because it wasn't yet serious enough, she didn't use her lights or siren.

Hopefully Lydia would turn up without making things official.

When she disconnected with Grimes, she called Sam and broke the news that she wouldn't make it for Saturday evening date night.

"Tell Alice she's taking my place," Taylor told him, but immediately remembered that she was going ice skating with the other kids.

"I'll be fine. Lonely, but fine," Sam said, sounding pitiful.

"I promise, I'll make it up to you," Taylor said, then said her goodbyes and hung up. If Sam wanted to be her husband, he was going to have to get used to canceled plans. That was part of the job, and she didn't like it either, but that's what she signed up for as law enforcement.

Alice had settled in nicely with Sam. Taylor had called in an owed favor from Wesley at Family Services, and he'd used his connections to grant Sam emergency temporary custody while a hearing was set. The DNA test was sent off, and now they waited. Life had gotten complicated after Cate's near death, Jo's crisis, and the appearance of Alice in their lives, but, so far, Taylor was holding it all together. Maybe by a thread, but that was better than nothing.

As she drove to the Walmart, her mind raced with thoughts of Lydia. Caleb Grimes was the newest addition to their department. He used to be a teacher, following in the footsteps of his father and grandfather. She'd heard that, when he taught, he was well loved by his students, but his heart had always been set on law enforcement. Finally, after a long career as an educator, he'd finally decided to chase his dream and become part of the sheriff's department.

At first, he'd worked part-time while juggling other jobs to support his family. Substitute teaching was one of them, and that kept him busy enough. But his dedication and determination had paid off, and when McElroy was fired, Grimes took his full-time deputy position. Now he was a valuable member of the team, a true asset to the department.

Good timing, too, since he and Lydia had surprised everyone by announcing they were pregnant again. They'd decided they weren't done building their family after all and little Zoey was born. Now Grimes was the proud—and busy—dad of three beautiful daughters, and it was no wonder his hair had grayed early, a nice salt and pepper look that added to his already outdoorsy appearance. With his thick hair and neat beard, he was handsome, but she knew from experience that having a houseful of daughters could be stressful.

His wife, Lydia, was gorgeous. The guys always teased Grimes that he'd married above his pay level, especially because Lydia was a therapist of some sort before she'd recently left her job to stay home with the baby. The truth was, they made a great couple and some of the guys were just jealous.

When Taylor arrived at Walmart, she found Grimes waiting near the entrance, his expression etched with worry. She pulled her cruiser up to him and put down the window.

"Thanks for coming, Taylor," he said, his voice tight with concern. "I appreciate it. I'm just worried. I have a bad feeling."

Taylor nodded in understanding. "Always trust your gut. Let's start by checking the parking lot. Maybe we'll spot her car. Is she still driving the old Suburban?"

Grimes nodded. "Yeah. Black, and it's got that silly family sticker on the back."

"I'll take the left side. Meet you back up here." She rolled away and went to the far side of the lot, then began combing through the rows, one by one.

Nothing. Taylor even drove around the building again, taking extra time to get out of the car where the cardboard boxes were stacked on pallets. It was cold for November, but she didn't care. She checked every corner and doorway, a few of them twice.

Finally, she had to give up. Neither Lydia nor her vehicle were anywhere to be found. She met Grimes at the end of the parking lot near the street this time. They pulled up, window to window. He looked even more worried.

"We need to pull the parking lot footage," Taylor suggested.

He shook his head in frustration. "Already tried. The store manager must do it and he doesn't come in until morning."

"Okay, well, I'm sure she's fine. Maybe her car broke down and her phone went dead. Let's expand our search," Taylor suggested. "She could've run into someone she knows. Or she might've gone to another shop. You take the north part and go east. I'll take the south and go west. Or what if she stopped in to see Mabel and have a drink on her day off from the kids?"

He shook his head. "No way. But, just in case, I'll check The Den parking lot next."

"No, I'll take that one. I need to stop in anyway. See if my dad is there," she said.

Grimes glanced at Taylor, his eyes filled with a mix of worry and determination. "I just hope she's okay, Taylor. She's my whole world. Hell, she's the whole world to all of us. The girls are worried, too. Grace said that Zoey has been crying nonstop for two hours, wanting her mama."

That thought stabbed Taylor in the heart. Those kids needed Lydia to come home. "Then let's find her, Grimes. If it takes all night, we'll keep looking."

CHAPTER 3

Taylor sat among her colleagues in the conference room at the sheriff's office. The room was dimly lit, with a whiteboard at the front and a long wooden table surrounded by chairs. Sheriff Dawkins stood at the head of the table, marker in hand, ready to lay out the plan for the search for Lydia Grimes. Today he'd skipped his creased khakis and button-down shirt, trading them for a more casual look of jeans and a black department polo shirt, his badge shining from where it was pinned. It looked like he hadn't slept much either.

She should know. She'd had him on the phone at two in the morning, waking him from a dead sleep and telling him that she had a gut feeling this wasn't a false alarm. The thing about the relationship between her and the sheriff was that he trusted her gut.

Sometimes more than she did.

Shane, Grimes, and several other deputies were also present. Everyone had coffee or a soft drink at hand, along with paper and pen, ready to snap into action. No one was making small talk or doing the usual pre-meeting antics and jibing.

Taylor had called Penner and Kuno to help, and they assisted

Grimes in a search from one side of the county to the other the night before. They hadn't found a trace of Lydia or her vehicle. All calls and texts went unanswered, and something told Taylor this was serious—women like Lydia Grimes didn't just drop off the face of the earth without warning.

Word had already spread through the department like wildfire and even those not scheduled to come in were there, ready to support their brother-in-arms. It was a tense atmosphere. Anxiety hung heavy in the air as they awaited the sheriff's directives.

Taylor glanced at Grimes, who sat beside her. His normally chill demeanor was shattered, replaced by raw worry etched into his face. His eyes were red, and his hands trembled as they clenched and unclenched. He looked ready to explode out of his chair, and she imagined it was damn hard to sit there when his wife was out there somewhere, possibly hurt or lost.

But they all knew the best way to find her now was a team effort.

Sheriff Dawkins began to write on the whiteboard, laying out the search strategy. His tone was professional and authoritative. No playful banter in sight.

"Alright, folks," he began, his voice commanding attention. "As you've heard, we've got a missing person case on our hands, and it's one of our own. I know it's early in the game—much sooner than we usually get involved—but Lydia Grimes is part of this department's family, and we're going to treat her disappearance with the utmost urgency. Gray, what's been done so far?"

She sat straighter in her chair. "Lydia was last heard from when she was leaving Walmart to do some more shopping. She didn't say where, just that she'd be home in a few hours. We searched the parking lot and found nothing. Then we did a street grid search last night, all the way up until the wee hours of the morning. Dottie called the hospitals in our county and the surrounding. All calls to Lydia went straight to voicemail, texts unanswered. Grimes called Lydia's sister and her mom, and the few friends she talks to on a regular basis."

He proceeded to detail the plan, assigning teams to various search areas, checking security footage from nearby businesses, and reaching out to Lydia's friends and acquaintances. The room was filled with the clatter of chairs and the rustling of paper as everyone took notes on their assignments.

Taylor listened intently, absorbing every detail of the plan, but her thoughts kept drifting to Grimes. She knew him well enough to understand the agony he was going through.

The fear of the unknown, the helpless feeling of not being able to protect someone you love—it was a gut-wrenching experience.

"Grimes, this might be a long shot, but I want you to pull every file from every perp you've arrested this year. See if any ring a bell of being overly pissed off at you."

Grimes nodded and made a note on his pad.

"And have you checked your banking accounts yet? See where else the cards were used?" Sheriff wrote banking on the board, then gestured at Penner. "Get up here and take notes, please."

Penner jumped to his feet and took the marker, then scribbled a bulleted list of things the sheriff had said so far.

"No. I'll call the bank when they open," Grimes said. "Lydia pays the bills, and I can't remember our online password. Also, the manager at Walmart had a problem pulling the parking lot footage, but he's got his tech guy coming in to help him. We should have that soon."

Taylor felt a rush of irritation. It never failed that when they needed video surveillance quickly from a business, either cameras were down, or the employees didn't know how to access the playbacks. It slowed everything down in an investigation. It couldn't be helped, though. Small town businesses didn't have the payroll for full-time security teams.

"Social media?" Sheriff asked, looking at Grimes. "Any digital check-ins reported?"

"She doesn't have time for social media," he said. "She hasn't touched it since the baby came. Grace uploads all the photos to our family profile, but Lydia rarely goes on there."

Penner wrote furiously.

"I want you to set a point person who will report back and forth to you for questions, Grimes. Someone you trust to talk for you. Usually it's a family member," Sheriff said. "If we don't find her today, things might get crazy, and you'll need a spokesperson."

"I'll call her sister and ask her to come." Grimes made a note.

"We need to get her phone records. See who she was texting or talking to yesterday," Shane said. "Every man thinks he knows everything about his wife, until they realize they don't."

Taylor kicked Shane under the table. He was such an ass sometimes.

He kicked her back, and it hurt.

She glanced at Grimes just in time to see his emotions seem to reach a breaking point. His breath hitched, and he abruptly stood up, knocking his chair back. He hurriedly mumbled an apology and made his way to the door, his eyes blurred with unshed tears.

Taylor excused herself and quietly followed him into the hallway.

She found him leaning against the wall, his shoulders shaking with silent sobs. She didn't care how unprofessional it was. He was more than a colleague. He was a friend, and he needed a friend's comfort.

Without a word, she wrapped her arms around him in a consoling embrace.

"Grimes," she whispered softly, "Don't listen to Shane's bullshit. He's an idiot."

He pulled back and his eyes were bloodshot from crying and lack of sleep.

"Lydia and I don't have secrets. And she'd never leave the baby. Or the girls. She wouldn't, Taylor." He sounded like he was pleading.

"I know, I know. She's a great mom," Taylor said.

"I swore to the girls that I'd bring her home, Taylor. Grace and Ella are freaking out. I gave my word." His voice shook and he hit the wall with his fist, leaving a slight indention.

Taylor nodded encouragingly. "Good. Because we'll find her. You hear me? We won't stop until we do. Lydia's part of this family and we take care of our own."

He looked like he wanted to say more but he didn't. After a few deep breaths, he wiped his eyes with the back of his hand. "Thanks, Taylor," he managed to say, his voice choked with emotion.

"You ready to go back in?" she asked.

He nodded and she followed him in. They took their seats again.

Taylor's slight bad feeling began to grow exponentially.

The sheriff gave a few more directives, then closed the meeting.

"Gray, stay behind. I need to talk to you," he said.

Everyone filed out and Taylor's stomach clenched. What had she done now to be singled out? She did a quick mental check of things he'd asked for lately. All of it was handed in.

Unless she was forgetting something.

Once the room was clear, he closed the door and propped himself on the corner of the table. His expression softened.

"How is Cate doing?"

Taylor's stomach unclenched and she took a deep breath, grabbing the closest chair.

"Much better, but she's got a long way to go. Thanks for asking."

"Is she getting up and around good now?"

"Some days yes, some days no. She's about to start some more strenuous physical therapy to help build the muscle back in her shoulder."

"What about Jo?" He looked even more concerned.

Taylor leaned back in her chair. "That one is more complicated. I almost think it's going to be easier for Cate to heal from her physical injuries than it will for Jo to get past this emotional punch. Eldon had her fooled. She thought they were going to build a future together, and all along he was harboring a hatred for our family. It sucks and she's having a hard time."

"Damn. There's some real evil in this world. I wish he was still alive so we could see him behind bars. He got off easy."

"Yeah, but that's another thing. My dad is nervous that this is going to come back and bite him in the ass."

Sheriff shook his head. "Nope. Self-defense. Straight up. Believe me, I'd have heard about it if they were going to take it further. That investigation will be closed by the end of the month. I guarantee it."

"I hope so."

The state police oversaw the investigation because Taylor was involved and a peace officer. So far, it had gone like they'd hoped, but you never knew when someone might throw in a wrench. Taylor waited every day to see if Eldon's mother, Blanche, would contact her, but so far she'd shown that she wanted to keep a low profile. Of course, she'd been brought into the investigation, too. Taylor had told the state police everything, and she assumed they'd interviewed Blanche, but didn't know for sure.

"That's not the only reason I wanted to talk to you alone, Taylor."

Uh-oh. When he used her first name, that usually meant she was in trouble.

"What's up?" She tried to sound nonchalant.

"I need a favor." He shifted on the table, looking uncomfortable.

"What kind of favor?"

"It's big. And it's personal, so I need your word that the details of the arrangement stay between us—and if things go like I want—your mother."

Taylor felt more unease. What could have to do with Cate that the sheriff would ask a favor for? Of course, he knew her, but not on a private level.

"Okay," she said, dreading his next words.

He sighed, looking miserable. Whatever it was, he didn't want to ask it.

"Fine," he said, throwing his hands up helplessly. "I'll just come out with it. This is embarrassing, but I have a niece who's in a lot of trouble. Her name is Sutton Scott and she's a nurse and a caregiver. She's been accused of stealing over thousands of dollars from her elderly patient. She's been indicted by a grand jury and she's facing multiple charges of elder abuse and fraudulent transactions."

"I'm sorry to hear that," Taylor said. "But what is the favor?"

She'd never heard him mention a niece named Sutton. Not that she knew everything about his family, but the name didn't ring a bell at all.

"First let me tell you, Sutton is not a bad person. She made a bad mistake, and I can hardly believe she did this, but, deep down, she's not a criminal She has only me, and I promised I'd look after her a long time ago. I've done a piss-poor job of it, obviously, or she'd have never gotten into this situation. I bonded her out, but I need someone to take her under their wing until her trial date. Keep her out of trouble and set her up with something to keep her busy that she can go to the courts with. Something positive."

"I'm not following, Sheriff."

He ran his hands through his hair and looked close to being sick.

"Just tell me," Taylor said, completely confused.

"She's not allowed to go back to work yet. Not officially.

Possibly never, if this goes the wrong way in court. So, I want to see if you can talk Cate into letting my niece stay with her and help her through the next few months. Be her caregiver. Take her to therapy. Work with the rescue animals. Anything that will help us get her probation when she's convicted. Because she will be convicted, I already know that."

Taylor was speechless. He wanted her to ask her mother to harbor a soon-to-be felon. That was a huge request for anyone. Why Cate?

Then it hit her.

Because Cate had done prison time, she was the best option. At least in his eyes.

She started to feel a bit perturbed, but then she remembered the young Taylor. The desperate one, going to school and working a minimum wage job. The one who didn't have a decent future to hope for until the Sheriff stepped up and gave her one. Until he told her he believed in her and that she'd be a good cop, if she set her mind to it.

Sheriff Dawkins had made her dreams come true. She was doing the job that she was meant to do, with all the passion that having someone believe in you could give. If she didn't have her badge, and the people of Hart's Ridge to protect, she didn't know what she'd do.

There really wasn't any question. The sheriff had never asked her for a favor. In all the years since they'd come together, and he'd rescued her.

"Okay. I'll talk to her, and I'll find a way to make it work," she said, trying to sound confident. Cate was a loner, and she already knew it wasn't going to be easy.

His immediate smile was filled with relief, as though a weight had been lifted from his shoulders. A weight exchanged for a long-overdue favor. Now Taylor was going to have to talk Cate into helping her pay back that favor.

"I can't thank you enough, Taylor. One more thing. I can't get her to reveal to me why she took the money. I know there must be something behind it. If you or Cate could get her to open up and tell you, then I might be able to help her more. Right now, her lawyer doesn't know how to defend her. She's giving him nothing."

"Ten-four. I'll bring Cate up to date on the situation. But, Sheriff, are you sure that she's safe? I mean, to stay with my mom? I can't jeopardize Cate's well-being or recovery, no matter how much I want to help. She may have spent years behind bars, but she's not the tough convict some might think. Especially now."

He held his hand up. "Scout's honor. Sutton is a good girl. I swear, she will be a lot of help. But, listen, let's wrap this up because I want you and Weaver to bring Lydia home to her family. Get on it and I want you to report back in two hours. Tell me what you've got. I'll send you Sutton's information and we can figure out when to make the transfer."

Transfer?

It sounded like he was handing over a prisoner, and Taylor had a sinking feeling that she was offering to do something that was going to be more difficult than the sheriff was letting on.

CHAPTER 4

Up until this moment, Cate couldn't recall a single instance when she'd been angry at one of her daughters. Sure, there must've been times when they were small children, before she'd had to go away, but she didn't remember any and hoped they didn't either.

But, right now, she was furious.

"How could you tell him yes for me? I don't want to be responsible for anyone, Taylor," she said, leaning forward in her chair. Either the exertion or her anger was causing her shoulder to ache, and she winced quietly.

She'd been claiming her pain was nearly gone, just so they'd stop asking about it.

"I'm sorry," Taylor said, pleading with her voice and her eyes. "I know it was wrong. It's just that the sheriff has never asked me for anything before, and I owe him so much. He stepped in as a father figure when Dad couldn't or wouldn't."

"I thought Cecil was your father figure?"

"Him, too. But the sheriff gave me the opportunity to make something of myself. I wouldn't have my badge if it wasn't for his support. Mom, if you do this for me, I'll never ask anything again. I swear it."

Cate glared at her.

The endearment got her, and Taylor probably knew it.

Most mothers didn't even think about being called *mom*. It was a normal thing that they took for granted. But it had taken decades for Cate to hear that word applied to her again. For years she'd only dreamed of being their mom again. Even if for only one second before she died. Since the incident and being shot, all the girls were calling her *mom* and every time Cate heard it, it was like a gift.

An undeserved one, no doubt, but one all the same.

"Tell me about her," she said through gritted teeth.

"I don't know much. We've been busy with the Grimes' case, so I only have the basics. She's a home health nurse and she's been arrested for stealing money from the account of one of her elderly patients. She has a grand jury indictment with several charges."

Cate shook her head. The only thing worse than a child abuser—in her book—was a thief. In prison, the thieves were marked for being scum. They had few friends, other than each other. As an OG—one of the longest-residing inmates—if someone got caught stealing from another inmate, they were brought in front of her a lot, and she had to decide their punishment based on the severity of the offense.

What she'd learned over the years was that once a thief, always a thief. Even when they repented and swore to never do it again, they usually did. She didn't know if it was the thrill or adrenaline rush they got from getting something that they didn't earn or didn't belong to them, or if they were just mentally ill, but thieves were a type of criminal that she despised.

"Married? Children? Age?" she asked, keeping her judgment to herself.

"I'm sorry. I don't know."

"Do you even have a last name? Or are you planning to plunk down a stranger in my house who we both know nothing about?"

Taylor looked surprised at her harsh words. Cate didn't soften them. She was being pushed into a corner and she didn't like that feeling. It brought back too many memories.

"Scott. Sutton Scott. I looked her up but she's not on Facebook. She also doesn't have a criminal history. I mean, other than this situation. Not even a traffic ticket. I even ran her nationally. No other arrests."

"You mean to tell me that Miss Snow White is suddenly a felon, and it came out of nowhere? She took advantage of an elderly person, stealing from them, but she's never had a bit of trouble before this *situation*, as you call it?"

Cate didn't buy it. The woman was facing a grand jury trial. This wasn't a simple misdemeanor or slap on the wrist.

"It appears so," Taylor said, looking hopeful.

"Look, Taylor," Cate said, taking a deep breath. "I'm not going to lie to you. I think this is a bad idea and you know I'm not a fan of strangers. I like to keep to myself, and, other than my family and my dog, I'm just fine being alone most of the time."

She didn't mention Ellis. That hadn't worked out like she'd thought, and it gutted her, but it was what it was. Her marriage had also fallen apart, due to tragedy, and Jackson needed to get it through his head that it was dead with no chance of coming back to life.

She sighed, long and hard. "But I will do this for you. Why? Because you really don't ask anyone for anything, so this tells me that this means a lot to you."

"Mom, thank you," Taylor said, visibly relaxing.

"I'm not promising she can stay here for as long as your sheriff wants her to. Trial or whatever. I'm only saying that we'll try it. If she's a psychopath, or a pain in my rear, the deal's off. That's all I can do. Take it or leave it."

"I'll take it," Taylor said. "I really need to get back to work. Can I bring her tomorrow?"

Against everything Cate's gut was telling her, she nodded her approval.

"But she's not getting my bed. Hope she can climb a ladder," she said.

Taylor smiled in agreement, thanked her again, and went out the door.

Cate sat back in her chair and crossed her arms over her chest.

Tomorrow was going to be a peculiar day. She was going to be stuck with a stranger and, because of her injury, there wasn't much she could do or anywhere she could disappear to. It was going to be close quarters. Awkward, to say the least. Cate had never thought she'd have another cellmate in this lifetime.

Turns out, God was quite a comedian.

CHAPTER 5

Taylor was barely settled in at her desk when she was called into Shane's office. She had a bad feeling as she walked down the hallway, her footsteps echoing on the tiled floor. When she entered Shane's office, she found the sheriff already there, his face pinched with concern as he stood behind Shane's desk, both of their attention pointing toward the computer monitor.

"Taylor, have a seat," Sheriff said, motioning to a chair in front of Shane's desk.

She took a deep breath and sat down, her heart pounding in her chest. "What's going on? Is everything okay?"

Sheriff exchanged a glance with Shane before speaking. "We've received the surveillance footage from Walmart," he began. "We need you to take a look at it."

Taylor furrowed her brow, her stomach churning with dread. She got up and moved around Shane's desk, next to the sheriff.

Shane hit the keyboard and the video began to play.

As she watched the footage, her heart sank. It showed a woman who was obviously Lydia leaving the Walmart store and pushing a shopping cart filled with bags to her car. She clicked her key fob and opened the hatchback. She loaded the bags inside, closed it, then returned her shopping cart to a corral.

She walked back to her car and, once again, hit her key fob.

Everything seemed normal until she opened the driver's door.

Right at that moment, two men came rushing toward her vehicle. One went to the passenger side, and the other for the driver's door while Lydia tried to fight him off, pushing at him, then trying to get her leg out to kick him.

Taylor's eyes widened in shock as she watched the struggle unfold on the screen. But the man overpowered Lydia and got in. Then from the little bit of shadow Taylor could see, appeared to drag Lydia over the console to his side so his partner could get in.

It took less than four seconds, and the doors were shut, Lydia trapped inside.

Taylor gasped as they sped away from the scene. Unfortunately, the camera was too far away to give them a good picture, but you could obviously tell it was two men, and what they'd done. She couldn't even imagine how terrified Lydia must have been.

She turned to the sheriff, trying to keep her voice from trembling. "Who were those men? What happened to Lydia? Where did they take her?"

He sighed heavily. "We don't know yet, but we're going to find out. We need to identify them and track them down."

Shane chimed in, "Grimes is already here, Taylor. Sheriff wants you to break it to him, then bring him in. He needs to see this. Maybe he'll recognize the men."

Taylor nodded, her heart aching for her friend and colleague. "Of course, I'll go talk to him right away."

"About what? Did you find her?"

They all turned to find Grimes standing at the door. He'd opened it so quietly they hadn't heard him. He had a young woman with him.

"This is Lydia's sister, Blair Ramsey," he said.

She nodded silently.

Taylor could easily see the resemblance, except Lydia was much taller.

"Nice to meet you, Ms. Ramsey. Caleb, come in and sit down," Sheriff said, looking suddenly sick with the knowledge that he was going to have to break the news himself.

Grimes looked at them, his gaze jumping from one to the other.

He stepped inside the room and pulled a chair out, then gestured for his sister-in-law to take it. She slid in quietly.

Grimes turned his attention back to the sheriff. "I don't want to sit. Tell me what happened."

Shane gestured for him to come around the desk. "Come look at this. I got the footage from Walmart, and it's not good, man."

The blood seemed to drain from Grimes' face, but he came around the desk and Shane hit the start button again.

As Grimes watched Lydia's figure push her shopping cart out the doors where the parking lot camera picked her up, he didn't move a muscle. But when it got to the part where the men overtook her, then took off with her in her car, his legs buckled, and he caught himself with his hands on the desk.

Shane stood and guided him into his chair.

"I know it's a bad quality, but do you recognize the men?" he asked.

Grimes could only shake his head as he stared at the last frame, his wife's vehicle exiting the parking lot.

"Let me see," Blair said, coming around the desk to peer at the screen. She watched, shaking her head. "Can't see them well enough to know who they are."

"They took her," Caleb said, his voice monotone and sounding lost.

"We'll find her," Taylor said, not letting her fear affect her words. Grimes needed to see them being strong and confident.

"Damn straight we will," Sheriff said.

"Are there any better images of the men?" Grimes finally asked, his voice shaking.

"Not on this piece," Shane said. "The manager is going over any internal footage that shows Lydia shopping or in line at the checkouts. He's going to send it over so we can analyze it to see if she was targeted from inside the store first. Hopefully we can get a clearer image of their faces."

Shane spoke up. "We've already got Penner making a list of businesses on the same road as Walmart and he's going to go see if they have any footage of the Suburban, hopefully to give an idea of which direction they were headed."

Grimes lowered his face into his hands and Blair put her hand on his shoulder. He'd picked the right family spokesperson, because she was obviously not allowing her emotions to get the best of her. She appeared to be more concerned for him.

Caleb, on the other hand … watching his feelings play out was brutal.

Taylor felt helpless. She didn't know what to say.

This was bad.

Very bad.

One moment Lydia was enjoying an evening away from her kids—just a mom out shopping and planning Christmas—and the next minute, her life and that of her family's was turned upside down.

"You should go home and be with your girls," Shane said. "That's your job right now."

"I agree," said the sheriff. "You go where you're needed the most right now and let us do our job."

"You're right," Grimes said. "I need to go home. I don't want the girls to hear about this from anyone else."

"I'll stay in touch with you every step of the way," Taylor promised him.

He locked eyes with her, a silent plea penetrating between them.

It made a lump appear in Taylor's throat.

She nodded back at him. Her promise not to keep anything back.

"Once we get clear shots of the men, we'll do a press conference and blast it everywhere," Sheriff said. "Someone must recognize them. If we can identify them quickly, Lydia will have a chance."

CHAPTER 6

It was only seven in the morning and Cate didn't know what to think of Sutton Scott. She'd expected someone younger, perhaps in their late twenties. Someone young enough to have done something so stupid as to steal from her patients, not a woman of around forty years old, give or take.

Sutton was petite. Much shorter than Cate. She wore her dark hair in a loose, casual style that fell on her shoulders. Not much makeup, just some mascara and lip gloss. Cate could easily imagine her working in a hospital, standing at someone's bedside taking their vitals quietly and professionally, barely waking them to do so.

She appeared to be a no-nonsense personality type, which were Cate's favorite kind of people. Good thing, because Cate had only had a day to back out of her commitment before time slipped away and Taylor had arrived with her that morning at seven.

It was alarming to see a stranger on her doorstep, complete with a suitcase and a taped-up box. With a quick introduction and disappearance act from her eldest daughter, Cate found herself standing there in awkward silence with not a clue what to do next.

"You got the loft," Cate finally said. "Be careful on the ladder and don't bump your head. It was built for the grandkids but there're stacking cubes and some hooks up there for clothes. Clean sheets on the bed, too. What's in the box?"

"Medical supplies," Sutton said.

"I don't need any."

Sutton shrugged. "I might. Anyway, would you like some breakfast?"

"I had toast and a boiled egg two hours ago," Cate said. "I'm used to getting up early to feed our boarded pets and the rescues. I haven't gone back to my routine, but I still wake up right on time." She didn't mention her problem with insomnia. Sutton would already know too much about her health before it was over.

Sutton nodded, then went to the sink and started washing the few dishes there. Like Cate, she didn't seem to be much of a talker. Her entire aura was one of calmness and a hesitancy before she spoke. Could be nervousness, or just how she was. It was too soon to tell.

She also didn't look like the average thief, though Cate had learned during her time behind bars that you couldn't put a label on people. Some of the inmates who came in as the nicest and most eager to please ended up stealing you blind if you turned your back for a second.

Others you could spot as soon as intake dropped them off.

"Why don't you sit down and let's talk for a bit?" Cate said. She didn't want to have a conversation either, but, since they were going to be staying together in close quarters, they might as well get it over with. Luckily, she'd had her cabin built with a small loft over the living room in case the grandchildren wanted to come stay, so Sutton would at least have her own space. It wasn't private, but it was a bed, hooks for clothes, and a spot to get out of Cate's way when things got too awkward.

Sutton came and sat on the couch. She crossed her legs and looked at Cate expectantly.

"Did you do it?" Cate asked, getting to the point.

"Yes," Sutton said. "I did."

She got a point for honesty. Most thieves would go to their graves denying.

"Why?"

"I can't really say," Sutton said.

"You can't, or you won't?"

"Both," Sutton said, her tone polite. "I'm sorry. About that, and the fact that my uncle asked this of you. I know it's a lot and I really appreciate it. I don't want to go to jail. I'll do my best to work hard for you all here, and maybe that will go a long way in sentencing."

"Did you give the woman back the money?" Cate asked.

Sutton shook her head. "No. Not yet."

"So you still have it?" That surprised Cate.

"Not exactly. It's complicated." Sutton was wringing her hands, and Cate could see that sweat beads peppered her upper lip.

Cate sighed. It was too soon. But there was a story there; she could feel it.

"So do you have any experience with physical therapy?" she asked, changing the subject.

"Just the basics. But I can learn. And I can keep you on task. I'll drive you to your appointments, too."

"You have a driver's license?"

Sutton laughed, and it sounded light and almost lyrical.

"Yes, I have a driver's license. A perfect record, too. No tickets and no crashes."

"That's good to know. My body has been through enough. Don't think it can take any more for now."

"I understand. If you can walk me through your medication schedule, I can stay on top of that, too."

"I think I can handle that on my own," Cate said. "I stopped taking the narcotics two weeks ago, against doctor's orders. I stick to over-the-counter meds if I need them, but I have a high pain tolerance."

"Impressive," Sutton said. "I just hope you don't let yourself suffer. It's okay to take pain meds if you take them correctly."

Cate stood and stretched, declining to take the subject further.

She had done time with women who were such addicts that they'd do anything to score one tiny pill. She remembered some of the girls smoking Clone, contraband tobacco sprayed with roach spray, rolled up like a cigarette. Chemicals so bad they ate the brain, but women so desperate they didn't care about the long-term damage as long as it made them feel different for a few minutes.

She turned to Sutton. "Let's go take a walk around the farm. Taylor said you were going to help with my share of the chores."

"Yep. I'll do whatever needs doing."

They walked outside and Cate led her first to the boarding facility. Anna was already at the front desk, working at the computer. She looked up when the bell rang over the door.

The dogs in the gated areas around erupted into a chorus of barking.

"Anna, this is Sutton. She's going to be working with us for a few weeks or so," Cate said, raising her voice over the din.

"Enough!" Anna yelled at the dogs, and they went silent. "Sorry," she said, standing and coming around the desk, putting her hand out. "Nice to meet you. I'll be by later with the recipe and stuff to make Mom's smoothies. We're working on building her muscle back."

"Okay, sure," Sutton said. "And I've got a few additives that will help, too."

Cate felt the heat rise from her neck and fill her face. She hated being the center of attention.

"Ladies," she waved her hand in the air. "I'm standing right here. Please don't talk about me as if I'm laying in the bed dying."

Anna looked stricken.

"Oh, sorry," Cate said. "Too soon? Anna, I'm fine. And if I miss a smoothie or two, it's not going to kill me. I can make them myself, you know."

"You say that, but you won't," Anna replied, shaking her head. "If Sutton can't do it, I'll continue."

"No, I'll do it. No problem," Sutton said eagerly. She looked around the big area, focusing in on the two dogs that came to sniff her legs.

"That's Mutt and Jeff," Anna said. "They're my dogs."

"Cute duo," Sutton said, but she stepped back and clenched her hands over her chest.

She was right. They were cute. A Great Dane and a Chihuahua, and a total surprise to all of them when Anna adopted and brought them home from the shelter. The dogs were best buds, and it was funny to see the little dog when he picked a place to nap within the gangly limbs of the Dane.

"Teague and Wyn get off to the school bus okay?"

Anna nodded. "Yep. Teague tried to fake a cough and stay home, but I stood strong."

Cate laughed.

"Mine used to do that, too," Sutton said.

"Oh, you have kids?" Anna asked.

"Yes. I mean—they're grown now but I have two. Twin girls. They're twenty-two now and in their last year of college."

Cate wondered what they thought of their mom catching a felony charge. And did that mean that Sutton was married? Where was Mr. Scott in all the mess?

"Is this what I'll be doing?" Sutton asked, quickly changing the subject as she looked around. "Working with the boarded dogs?"

"No," Cate said. "Not at the counter for intake and pickup. Anna and Jo do most of that. They're the best with people out of all of us. Lucy takes care of marketing and advertising. She's our social media manager and event planner. I take care of feeding, cleaning, exercising—that kind of stuff. I get help from Taylor, and a few others. We all pitch in on the hard stuff."

"Sounds like a lot of hands-on work."

Cate nodded. "Yes. With our rescues, too. We've got two horses now, a llama, alpaca, and several birds. The rescue dogs are kept at another building that has kennels and outdoor runs. Like this one, but much smaller. This building also has our meeting room, a kitchen, a dog-washing room, and, of course, this nice lobby for intake and interaction with the customers. You and I will stick to the animals."

Sutton suddenly looked nervous.

"What's wrong?" Anna asked.

"Nothing, I'm good," Sutton said.

"You're afraid of dogs," Cate said. She'd already sensed it when Anna's dogs came running up to Sutton and she'd backed up and lifted her hands out of the way.

"I'll be fine. I'm sure."

She didn't look like she'd be fine. She looked like she'd be expected to pet rattlesnakes around the farm.

"You can do most of the tasks from the other side of a pen or gate, if you like," Cate said.

Sutton's shoulders dropped, and she looked relieved.

"That obvious, huh?" she said, then pointed to her upper lip. "See that scar? It's from a German Shepherd that belonged to my neighbor when I was a kid. Just snapped one day. Out of the blue. It's hard for me to trust dogs now, even if they're supposed to be tame."

Cate could see a barely visible line that ran from Sutton's upper lip to her nose.

"I'm so sorry that happened to you," Anna said.

"Don't worry," Cate said. "we don't keep aggressive dogs here. At least, not for long. All our boarded dogs are interviewed for behavioral issues before we agree to take them. And if a rescue turns out to be aggressive, it's kept separate from the other rescues until we can figure out if the animal can be helped. Sometimes it's just an issue of time and learning how to redirect their anxiety. I promise we won't put you in with any untested animals."

Sutton nodded. "Thank you. I don't want to be an inconvenience, though. I'm sure I'll be fine. I just appreciate you allowing me to be here."

A customer came through the door holding a squirming Yorkshire Terrier. Anna welcomed her and Cate took the opportunity to lead Sutton outside.

"Let me show you where the rescue dogs stay," she said.

As they walked, she pointed out the small goat yard, and the barn and small area where Apollo and the new horse hung out.

"They're all rescues?" Sutton asked.

"Yep. They come to us abandoned, or sometimes picked up because of neglect. We get them well, then rehabilitate, and hopefully find them a new family that will be their forever home."

They got to the smaller building and opened the door to find Jo inside, hosing down the kennels on the right. She turned and waved, attempting a slight smile.

The sadness she carried broke Cate's heart.

"That's Jo, another daughter. This afternoon when school's out, you'll see her son Levi around. He practically lives outside."

They walked the middle lane between the two rows of kennels and Cate introduced the dogs as they went, telling what she knew of their stories. When they got to the end, a Rottweiler came charging the metal door between them, snarling and barking. Cate put an arm out, urging Sutton to take a step back, though it wasn't needed because, when she looked, Sutton had retreated at least five feet further up the lane.

"He can't get to us," Cate called out to her.

Sutton came a bit closer, but she was obviously terrified.

Cate said. "We named him Zeus. He probably wouldn't do anything. He's just scared, so he's acting out. He was found with the chain to his neck wrapped around a telephone pole downtown last weekend in the pouring rain. Only had about a foot of length to look around. Couldn't move otherwise. We think he was used to sire puppies for a backyard breeder."

"That's so sad," Sutton said.

"And common. As long as people keep buying them, we'll never snuff out those responsible for so much animal cruelty."

"What do I need to do to help?" Sutton said, suddenly looking worried. "You look like you're wearing down. Maybe you should go back and rest."

Cate didn't want to, but Sutton was right. And observant. The walk was the furthest she'd done so far, and the effort was starting to make itself known.

She pointed at the other end of the rows of kennels. "There's a hose on that end, too. On my way out I'll tell Jo to show you how to send the dogs to their patios and lock down the doors so you can clean their kennels. You can meet her in the middle and get it done quickly, then help her with whatever else she says."

"Ten-four, Boss," Sutton said.

Cate didn't have the energy to correct her. She needed to get back to her cabin. Maybe later she'd explain to Sutton that she was done being anyone's boss. That ended when she was set free, and she'd nominated someone else to oversee the prison garden center.

CHAPTER 7

Taylor was waiting at the door to the bank when the branch manager, Denosha Evans, a stunning black woman with an air of confidence, arrived and opened the lock, then led her inside. The bank's interior was a small, tidy space with a neat row of teller windows, plush leather chairs, and polished marble floors. The early morning sunlight streamed in through the large windows, casting a warm glow over everything.

They still had half an hour before it was open to the public but hopefully would find what Taylor needed before then.

"I'm so sorry to hear about all this," Denosha said, then led the way to her office and gestured for Taylor to have a seat. She went around to her computer and started booting it up. "My daughter goes to school with Ella, so I know the family by more than just banking. How are the girls doing?"

"Not good," Taylor replied. "All they know so far is that their mom is missing, so, please, the rest of this needs to remain confidential until after the press release."

"Of course." Denosha didn't even look up as she worked.

Caleb had called Taylor as soon as the transactions had come through, and it was bad. Two withdrawals of five hundred each. One was made only minutes before the call Lydia made to Grace to tell her she was fine and was going to do more shopping. The other withdrawal just that morning. Now they needed to see who had made it.

"Okay, I've got it up and ready, if you want to pull your chair around," Denosha said.

Taylor dragged her chair next to Denosha's and leaned in toward the screen.

"I know which machine and camera it was, so that makes it quicker, but I'm going to have to just play through each transaction until we get to the stamped time," Denosha said.

"That's fine. I just hope we get something."

Walmart had turned up nothing else, other than the first grainy footage showing the men hustling Lydia into the car. They'd obviously not followed her into the store, or found her there first, because she and Penner had looked through every shot of Lydia on every aisle she visited. She'd had no one on her tail inside.

"It might just be Lydia, but let's see what we got," Denosha said, moving through frames quickly.

Taylor recognized most of the people who came through and used the drive through machine. A few she didn't, and when Denosha got to the time of the first withdrawal, at first Taylor thought the next man on the screen was just a local.

"This is the transaction under Lydia's card," Denosha said.

But it wasn't Lydia.

"Who is that?" Taylor said, almost to herself, as dread flooded through her veins.

"No one I've ever seen." Denosha said.

It was a man. Not an attractive one, either. He was nearly bald, and his skin was so pale it was nearly transparent. He looked nervous, which was to be expected considering he was using someone else's bank card. He put the pin number in once, and when it was denied, he shouted over his shoulder, paused, and put it in again.

This time it went through.

"Freeze it right there," Taylor said, then took a few screen shots of the man's face. "Okay, let it go."

They watched him grab the cash, then drive away quickly. No one else could be seen in the car, but Taylor saw shadows that indicated there were at least two more people with him. She hoped that one of them was Lydia. That would mean she was at least alive.

"That's all of it," Denosha said. "I'll send this to your email address,"

She pushed a notepad toward Taylor. "Jot it down here."

Taylor did that and noticed her hand was shaking. Every fiber in her being said that Lydia was in deep trouble, and they needed more manpower. She was going to tell the sheriff that, too. She thought about Sissy, and how she'd disappeared, murdered at the hands of the one who proclaimed to love her so much. Then she thought of Caleb, and of course she wondered for an instant if he was as dumbfounded about Lydia's disappearance as he claimed to be.

That was the funny thing about crime, though. Sometimes the person you trust the most turned out to be the most dangerous. It happened all the time. Laci Peterson and her unborn child, murdered by her supposedly loving husband. LaToyia Figueroa and her unborn son, too. Yet again, two strangled and lost by the baby's father. Pregnant Shanann Watts and her beautiful two daughters, four lives wiped out by her husband, the daddy who said his daughters were his whole world. That such evil lived in the world, posing as normal human beings up until the moment the world realized they're monsters, is a horrible thing to dwell on and Taylor tried to shake it off.

That was not going to be Grimes.

"Thanks, Denosha. I'll be in touch if we need anything else."

The email had already come through when she got into the car and she forwarded it to Shane, then called him.

"Where're you at?" he answered.

"Headed there now from the bank. Just forwarded you the footage. Lydia didn't make the second transaction, but she may have been in the car. It was a man, and Denosha and I have never seen him before."

"Was there any sign of violence in the car during the transaction?"

"No," Taylor said. "It was silent other than the machine noises."

There was a long pause before Shane answered.

"We have to take into consideration that she may not want to be found," he said. "Could be a lover. Maybe they're running away together. Busy husband. Three kids. Could be that Lydia is tired of her life."

"Everything is a possibility until we rule it out, but I'd bet my next month's salary that you're wrong on that one," she said.

"Email just came through," Shane said. "The press conference is in half an hour, so hurry back and do not talk to Grimes about this yet."

He hung up and Taylor pulled out of the parking lot and stepped on the gas.

Of course she wouldn't talk to Grimes yet. She wasn't a rookie, and Shane didn't need to tell her that, but perhaps since she and Grimes were such good friends, he thought it was necessary. He would need to know soon, and not only that but he could possibly ID the guy.

Taylor had promised him she wouldn't hold back anything, but first they needed to regroup at the department. Tell the sheriff what they had and get approval on how to handle it with Grimes.

She considered calling Sam to check in, but she was worried that he might be frustrated with her already for as much time as she'd been at work the last two days, and it didn't appear that she would have any time off again until Lydia was found and brought home. Sam was dealing with Alice on his own, having to figure out how to be a step-in parent, and that was hard for him. He also had all responsibilities of Diesel, and Taylor felt bad about how she'd been neglecting him, too. On top of that, Sam was waiting for the DNA report to come back about the paternity of Alice, and he was trying to make a living.

Things were tough for him right now, too, and Taylor couldn't even be there to help him balance it all out. The more she thought about it, the more she realized that she was terrible wife material. A mate with an unpredictable schedule who had to drop any and everything at a second's notice when a case came up—who would want to live with that? Wives did it all the time but, with the tables turned, could Sam even deal with a life like that? What about if they had children?

She glanced at the ring on her finger.

Taylor loved her job, and she still dreamed of being promoted to detective one day, but would Sam end up resenting her if they got married?

It was a lot, and, as she pulled into the department, she reminded herself that her priority right now was Lydia. It made her sad for Sam. And Diesel, and Alice, and even Cate and the rest of her family she was neglecting, but this was what she'd signed up for.

Feeling suddenly exhausted, she parked and made her way into the department.

THE CONFERENCE ROOM was buzzing with anticipation as Taylor and Shane flanked the sheriff at the front of the room, facing a sea of reporters, microphones, and cameras. There was a crew from Atlanta, lured in because this was a missing wife of a law enforcement officer, and they had the best position at the front of the room and were shooting live. The lights from the cameras were blinding and hot. Most of the department's employees were there, some in the room and others listening from the hallway.

The room felt smaller than it was, suffocating in its intensity.

Sheriff cleared his throat, his authoritative presence commanding attention. He began, "Ladies and gentlemen, thank you for coming today. I stand before you with a heavy heart to discuss a matter of great importance to our community, and especially to one of our own here at the department."

Cameras clicked and reporters leaned forward, their pens poised to capture every word.

"As you may be aware," Sheriff continued, "Lydia Grimes, a member of our community and a beloved wife and mother, has gone missing. She was last seen leaving a local Walmart parking lot on the night of November fifteenth. We are deeply concerned for her safety and well-being."

A chorus of questions erupted from the reporters, but Sheriff held up a hand to silence them, his stern gaze unwavering.

"We have reason to believe that Lydia may have been abducted, and we are doing everything in our power to locate her and bring her home safely," he stated firmly. "We are here today to ask for your assistance in this matter."

Sheriff gestured toward Shane, who clicked his remote to make the image of the stranger in Lydia's Suburban at the ATM machine pop up on the huge, white screen. Then Shane stepped to the mic, his expression determined.

"We would like to identify this individual and urge you to call in if you know who he is. It's imperative to investigating this case, and we are asking for the public's help. Also, if anyone was at the Walmart parking lot on the night of November fifteenth and witnessed anything unusual or saw this man in the area, we urge you to come forward and provide any information you may have."

Several hands shot up among the reporters, and Shane pointed to one of them.

"Where exactly was Lydia last seen?" a reporter asked.

Shane replied, "Lydia Grimes was last seen in the Walmart parking lot here in town. We are specifically interested in any witnesses who may have observed her or the two individuals we believe were involved in her disappearance, whether it was inside the store or in the parking lot."

Another reporter chimed in, "Can you provide a better description of Lydia's car, in case someone spots it?"

Shane nodded and gave a detailed description of Lydia's Suburban, including the make, model, color, and license plate number. He told them about the sticker on the back and urged anyone who had seen the car to contact law enforcement immediately.

Just as the questions continued to pour in, a commotion caught Taylor's attention. Dottie from dispatch hurried in the hallway toward the sheriff, her expression frantic. She whispered urgently to Sheriff, who turned his attention away from the reporters for a moment.

Dottie relayed the news, "Sheriff, we just received a call from someone watching the live press conference. He claims to have been kidnapped by the same man seen in the footage you just showed. He's holding."

Sheriff exchanged a quick glance with Shane before nodding firmly. "Thank you, Dottie. Let's get him on the line in my office immediately."

CHAPTER 8

Taylor sipped at her coffee, wishing she hadn't skipped adding a dollop of cream and a sugar packet. Black was needed though because she was tired. It was ten o'clock at night and she was still at the department, but things were moving fast. Though it was for a terrible reason, she was excited to be a part of her first FBI-involved case and to have not only one but two special agents there to help them sort through this crazy mess that was their investigation.

It had been three days since Lydia Grimes was carjacked and abducted. Taylor sat in the conference room, listening intently as Special Agent Mateo Lopez from the Atlanta FBI field office and Special Agent Andre Robbins from North Carolina went over their background and why they were sent to Hart's Ridge.

Her coffee had grown cold, nearly forgotten as she hung on every word.

Special Agent Robbins, sitting next to her, maintained a composed demeanor, his steely eyes focused on Shane as he spoke.

Shane, on the other hand, seemed less than pleased with the federal agents' presence. Taylor could practically see the tension radiating from him as he asked questions about jurisdiction. The agent from Atlanta was also a threat to Shane's alpha complex.

Special Agent Lopez was not only successfully fulfilling a very coveted position in law enforcement, but he was also tall, dark, and handsome, a combination of traits that Shane probably took as a threat to his reign as the department's most eligible—and sexiest, *at least in his own eyes*—employee.

Lopez spoke up, addressing Shane firmly, "Look, I'm not shutting you out. But this is going to be a federal case and it's much bigger than one missing woman."

Taylor exchanged a knowing glance with Sheriff, silently acknowledging that this was a matter that required their collaboration with the FBI, whether Shane liked it or not. She was also glad that Grimes wasn't there to hear that statement. He didn't even know yet that they had a lead, though Taylor had broken the news to him that a man driving Lydia's car used her card to make the bank withdrawals. He hadn't taken it well, but the sheriff ordered him to stay at home and wait for more intel.

Shane, still wearing a look of defiance, retorted, "I'll remain lead detective for our case."

Sheriff stepped in to defuse the brewing conflict. "We appreciate your help," he said to the agents diplomatically, but his stern glance was a clear reminder to Shane to cooperate.

Robbins reminded Taylor of a young Denzel Washington. He seemed unflustered by the tension, leaning back in his chair. He knew his position as the lead agent didn't need to be asserted verbally; it was understood. The room fell into a momentary silence, each person processing the gravity of the situation.

"We're still piecing together the timeline and their movements," Lopez continued, "but it's clear they pose a significant threat to anyone they come in contact with." Someone knocked at the door, and he rose and went to it, sticking his head out before closing it again.

"Hammond is out there now," he said. "Let's go over what we

know so far before we bring him in," he said, then started reading from his laptop screen. "On November 4, two inmates escaped from the Mecklenburg County jail by scaling a wall in the recreation center and leaving the area on foot. Inmate number one is a white male by the name of Billy Barnes who was serving the final years of a felony forgery conviction. Inmate number two is Avery Fisher who was in on first degree abuse of a child aged twelve years or younger."

Taylor couldn't help but wince when she heard the charges against Fisher. She couldn't imagine the horrors he was capable of.

"Where were the cameras? The supervisors?" Shane was incredulous.

"The inmates were unfortunately left unsupervised, and the security cameras weren't in their usual positions that day," Robbins said. "That's beside the point right now. They showed up thirteen miles away in Belmont, knocking on the door of John Hammond."

"Who is seriously lucky to be alive," Lopez added.

"Let's bring him in," Sheriff said. "I want to hear his experience straight from him. Deputy Gray, go get him."

Taylor did as she was told and found Hammond sitting in the front lobby, Dottie working late to watch him carefully as though he were the criminal, and not a victim.

"Follow me, Mr. Hammond," Taylor said.

Hammond looked anxious. From the camouflage clothing and the muddy boots he wore, it appeared that he was a hunter. He clutched his John Deere cap in his hands as he rose from his chair and trailed behind her. He was a big man with heavy footsteps. She couldn't imagine anyone overpowering him, but it happened.

In the conference room, she gestured for him to sit at the head of the table.

"John," Lopez greeted him and nodded. "Thanks for coming."

"You're welcome, Lopez. Wish I could say it's been a long time," Hammond returned.

"We appreciate you driving all this way tonight, Mr. Hammond," Sheriff said.

"No problem. You can call me John," he replied, running his hand through his hair nervously.

"John, you already know we are trying to catch up with Barnes and Fisher, but now we think they may be involved in a missing person's case here in town. A wife and mother by the name of Lydia Grimes went shopping and never made it home. We'd like you to tell your story, so those here investigating Mrs. Grimes case can get a feel for what we're dealing with."

Hammond nodded rapidly, his Adam's apple bobbing up and down.

"November the fifth, I was in my chair watching a game on TV when someone knocked on the door. I answered it, and it was Barnes, though I didn't know his name at the time. He said his car broke down and he needed to use my phone."

"He didn't have his own phone?" Shane asked.

Robbins gave him a peculiar look. "Phones aren't allowed in the detention centers."

Shane looked embarrassed for his lapse but nodded to Hammond to keep going.

"He made two calls, then asked me to take him to the closest store. When we stepped back outside, his buddy, Fisher, was out there. I was nervous but I'd already said yes, and I wanted them off my property and away from my family, so we all got in my truck and left." He paused, swallowing hard before continuing. "On the way to the store, Barnes was in the back seat, and he tells me that their car is broken down along the interstate in Gastonia and they need me to take them there instead. By then they were acting all kinds of weird, so I didn't say no. But, almost to Gastonia, they said their car was in Columbia, South Carolina!"

"What did you do then?" Lopez asked.

"I pulled over and told them to get the hell out," Hammond said. "Then Barnes reached up and put a knife to my neck. Pushed it in hard enough to draw blood, too." He reached up and touched the small bandage over his jugular. "Their niceties turned off like a light switch and they acted like they wouldn't mind killing me to get what they wanted."

"Next?" Shane asked, his tone bored.

"*Next*," Hammond said sarcastically, looking at Shane pointedly before directing his attention back to the sheriff, "I did exactly what they said. Kept driving until, about an hour later, they tell me to pull over. Fisher takes the wheel and gets off the interstate onto a highway. He drives to a field, pulls in, and makes me get out. I think they're going to kill me, but he orders Barnes to tie me to a tree with my own damned rope. But Barnes does it too slow and Fisher kicks him out of the way and finishes up. Then they leave."

"How did you get out of the situation?" Shane asked.

"It wasn't easy. Took me about four hours but I was determined to get loose before the coyotes came to check me out. I finally got the knots undone and walked to the highway. I flagged down a truck driver. He wouldn't let me in his cab, but he called the police. They took me to the station and told me they were already looking for two men on the run not too far away. Showed me photos of the inmates and, yep, it was them."

"Anything else to add?" Lopez asked him.

Hammond shook his head. "Nope. Just that they're dangerous. I feel sorry for anyone who gets in their way, and I hope you find that lady."

"Thank you, Mr. Hammond," Sheriff said. "I think you know the way out."

Robbins jumped to his feet and opened the door, telling Hammond he'd be in touch with him again in a few days. When he sat back down, he looked grim.

"That sounds scary enough, but it's just the beginning of their crime spree. It gets worse before they made their way to your town. We don't know all of it yet, but are you ready to hear some of what else they've been up to?"

Taylor steeled herself.

"Tell us what you know," Sheriff said. He looked defeated.

Taylor felt it, too. It was looking worse and worse for Lydia Grimes.

CHAPTER 9

At five thirty the next morning, Taylor returned to the department, having barely slept and feeling irritable because Lydia was still out there somewhere, possibly hurt. Taylor was also buried in guilt about Sam and Alice, especially after Alice had texted her several times the day before asking her when she'd be coming over. They hadn't told her about Lydia; she only knew that Taylor was working on a big case. To a twelve-year-old girl, it probably felt like Taylor had put her on the back burner, not important enough to be a priority.

It made Taylor feel terribly uncomfortable.

Sam was doing his best to smooth things over, but some of the texts he didn't even know about and really pointed to the fact that it was easier for Alice to have Taylor there as a buffer when things got awkward. She had to focus, though. Hopefully she'd be able to make it up to Sam, Alice, and even Diesel soon.

The big conference room was now base camp. Special Agent Robbins had gone back to North Carolina, but Lopez stayed behind and would be the main FBI contact, the eyes and ears and the one directing next steps.

They'd gone home late the night before and agreed to meet up again at seven this morning, so Taylor thought she'd be the first one there. But when she walked into the break room to get her first cup of coffee, the sheriff had beat her to the machine. If not for his freshly shaved face and the slight scent of Old Spice, she'd have thought he'd stayed there all night.

"Morning, Sheriff."

He nodded. "How are things going with Sutton and Cate?" he asked, taking his cup to one of the tables. He sat down heavily, and she could tell he was tired.

"To be honest, I don't know. I've barely been there, but, considering Cate isn't telling me to come get your niece and haul her away, I guess that's positive news."

He gave her a slight smirk.

Taylor had seen Sutton around the farm, headed into the barn and carrying oats out to the horses. Obviously, she was standing in for Cate for chores, but Taylor wondered too how it was going inside the cabin, where the square footage was smaller, and her mom didn't have anywhere to go to be alone.

"Grimes is coming in for an interview first thing this morning," he said next. "Lopez and Weaver will do it. I want you on the phone, following up on the tip line calls."

She tried not to show her surprise.

"I know you don't like it, but we have to consider him as a suspect," Sheriff said. "At least get it down on paper so the feds will get off my ass about him."

"I get it," she replied, then leaned against the counter where she could face him. Obviously, the agents didn't know anything about Grimes, and how devoted he was to his family. To Lydia. She couldn't expect them to go on her word alone that he was a good man. "But we already know for a fact that Barnes and Fisher took her."

"But we don't know if it was random or ordered by someone. Oh, and don't try to sneak in on the interview," Sheriff said. "You're too close to Grimes."

"Yes, sir." She wasn't going to push her luck. She and Grimes weren't best friends by any means, but if she made any ruckus, the sheriff might take her off the case.

"Is he bringing a lawyer?" she asked.

"Not that I know of. Should he?" Sheriff said.

"I have no idea," Taylor said. "Someone may have told him he needs one. His sister-in-law looked very protective over him when they were here."

"I guess we'll see," he replied.

Blair had been calling and texting Taylor regularly for updates. She was on top of things on the home front, too, reporting that she had reached out to over three dozen family members and friends to see if anyone knew anything. So far none of them did.

Taylor was glad she was there with Grimes and the girls.

The department was still fielding calls from the tip line as they tried to determine where Fisher and Barnes were now. One hope they held onto was that if the evil duo had dropped Hammond off unharmed, then maybe they'd done the same to Lydia. Getting to her on time was critical. The weather was supposed to turn bitter cold in the coming days.

Shane joined them and took a seat next to the sheriff. He'd brought in his own liquid breakfast, some sort of energy drink in a silvery can, and he set it down next to his binder.

"I miss anything?" he asked.

"Nope," Sheriff said.

Shane opened his binder. "Let's go over this again before Lopez gets here."

Taylor took a seat, not commenting on the sour note Shane used when referring to the agent. A few hours' sleep hadn't softened his attitude toward the man, it seemed.

"According to the rest of Robbins' report last night, after leaving Hammond tied up in the field, Fisher and Barnes drove to Myrtle Beach to visit one of Fisher's former girlfriends, Trixie

Simpson. On November the sixth, they abandoned Hammond's vehicle at a hotel and walked to a trailer shared by Simpson and her friend, Annette Riker. The four then drove to a hotel in Florence, South Carolina, and stayed there for the next few days. At some point, Barnes and Riker began a consensual sexual relationship." Shane paused and took a drink.

"Staying busy, aren't they?" Taylor said, filling the pause.

"Trying to keep moving to avoid being caught," Shane said, nodding. "During their time in Florence, Fisher asked Simpson if she knew anyone from whom he could obtain firearms. Simpson informed Fisher that a friend of hers kept several firearms at his home. The women thereafter agreed to lure the male friend out of his house by offering to buy him breakfast. While he was at breakfast with them, Barnes and Fisher entered his home and stole four firearms, a ring, and several blank checks. They then reunited with Simpson and Riker, and the four traveled in Simpson's van to Georgetown, South Carolina. That night, November 8, Barnes and Riker stayed at a hotel in town while Fisher and Simpson drove back to Florence to smoke marijuana and methamphetamines with Fisher's brother, Reggie Fisher, who claims to not know where they were headed to next."

"They're bouncing around without a plan," Sheriff said. "Only fools wouldn't know to lay low when the feds are after them."

Taylor agreed and she hoped they were fool enough to get caught. Like, today.

Shane continued. "The next morning, November 9, Barnes and Riker drove to a local store in Georgetown to purchase an assortment of snacks that they paid for with the stolen checks. Barnes talked to teenagers in the parking lot, and, according to Riker, he told her that they had some money and he wanted to kill them for it. He invited the teenagers back to the hotel room. Simpson and Fisher arrived back at the hotel shortly thereafter, and, luckily for them, the teenagers left unharmed."

"Where are the two women now?" Sheriff asked.

"On the morning of November 10, Barnes and Fisher left to go to town and never returned. The women were waiting at the hotel room in Georgetown, watching television when they saw the news about Hammond. They were scared they were going to go down for something the guys have done, so they called in and the local precinct picked them up. They're in custody in Columbia, South Carolina, now and are waiting to hear what charges if any will be filed against them," Shane said.

"Robbins interviewed them himself?" Sheriff asked.

Shane nodded. "Yes, and they're looking high and low for the vehicle. So far, no sign of it. Makes me think they've already left town. As it stands now, we don't know where the two men were from the morning of November 10 until they snatched Lydia Grimes on November 15 here in Hart's Ridge, and that's the last known sighting of them. They ditched the van somewhere and are now presumably in the Grimes' Suburban. We do know they're armed and dangerous."

Dangerous was right. Not to mention, criminals like them could do a lot of damage in five days. Taylor hoped there weren't any more victims involved. She held onto the fact that they'd left not only John Hammond—but also Trixie Simpson and Annette Riker—unhurt.

She prayed they'd do the same with Lydia.

"What else?" Sheriff asked, tapping his pen against the wooden tabletop.

"Lydia's phone records should be in this morning," Taylor said. "Hopefully we'll know who she called or texted that day and the days leading up. See if there are any secrets lurking."

"What about banking? Any more transactions?" Sheriff asked.

"No," Taylor said. "But Denosha is monitoring it closely."

"Friends or family hear from her that day?" Sheriff asked.

"Nope," Shane said. "We've talked to everyone on the list that Grimes gave us. Other than a few calls and texts between Grimes and Lydia that morning, then the one call that Grace picked up in which Lydia said she was going to be out longer shopping, she made no other attempts to contact anyone."

"Sounds about right."

They turned to find Lopez standing in the doorway, his arms crossed over his chest as he leaned on the frame. In his form-fitting black slacks and a black turtleneck, he looked like he was posing for an Eddie Bauer commercial.

"You're early," Shane said.

"Always," replied Lopez.

He might've been early, but he hadn't scrimped on cleaning himself up. His thick, black hair was styled perfectly, and he'd shaved close, showing just how chiseled his jaw was.

He looked more like a Latin rock star than an FBI special agent.

"We were early, too," Shane said, a competitive edge to his words.

You sound like an idiot, Taylor wanted to tell him, but she kept her mouth shut. No sense in adding fuel to the fire that was already brewing.

"Penner stopped me on the way in," Lopez said. "Seems the yoga instructor at the studio that Lydia goes to said they have one elderly gentleman in class who tried to get Lydia to go to coffee with him a few times. Said she always shut him down nicely but feels like it could be important."

He came to the table and handed Taylor a scrap of paper with a name on it. "She had his phone number and address from his file. Check it out today, would you?"

"Yes, sir," Taylor said, reading the name.

John Dellory

"We know John," she said, then turned to the sheriff. "It's John Dellory, the manager at Tractor Supply."

Sheriff nodded. "Good guy, but go clear him anyway."

"I will," she replied.

Lopez went to the cabinet and pulled a mug from it, then filled it with water and put it in the microwave.

"There's coffee already made," Taylor said.

"I drink herbal tea. Brought my own." He pulled a teabag from his pocket and dangled it, smiling at Taylor. "Ginger with Turmeric."

Shane ignored him and took a drink from his can.

Lopez pointed at it and scoffed. "Be careful with those. Harvard did a study and they found that drinking too many energy drinks can result in high blood pressure, irregular heartbeat, anxiety, and insomnia. Considering we must snatch our z's when we can, you might want to evaluate what you drink during the day. I can give you some tea."

"I'm good," Shane said, his attention suddenly on taking random notes.

"You think so, but you might regret those choices in the long term," Lopez said.

Taylor could feel the irritated vibes coming in waves from Shane and she knew Lopez could too. He seemed to like it.

As a matter of fact, they acted like they were in a pissing contest.

"We're just going over what we have so far on Barnes and Fisher," Sheriff said, moving the conversation along.

"I got the footage from the Georgetown Walmart," Lopez said. He talked as he got his mug out of the microwave and moved his teabag back and forth in the water. "They bought camouflage clothes. Fisher also stole a purse and cell phone from a customer in the parking lot. Female victim unhurt but shaken pretty badly."

Shane went to the board and jotted down what Robbins reported.

Taylor shook her head in disgust.

Barnes and Fisher were out of control and leaving havoc in their path.

They needed to get these guys off the street.

TAYLOR'S FINGERS tapped rhythmically on the keyboard as she logged the latest tip line calls. Each call, no matter how trivial it seemed, could hold the key to finding Lydia, and she remained methodical, knowing just one good lead might bring her one step closer to solving the case.

She stared at the big white board with all their notes and printed photos they'd stuck to it. She had followed up on all the tips so far. Most weren't valuable.

It was brutal.

Lydia's phone log had come in and there was nothing on it that looked unusual. All the calls and texts that she made were to family members and a friend at yoga class—the one who said she had no idea what had happened either.

Taylor had also confirmed that there was no GPS tracking on Lydia's car.

Dead ends. It was like Lydia Grimes had disappeared off the face of the earth. If they could only find Barnes and Fisher, that would probably lead them to her. The two men might be ignorant in some ways, but they were smart enough to keep changing vehicles, keeping authorities on their toes with what to look out for.

The clock on the wall seemed to tick agonizingly slow. Sheriff had stepped into his own office to take a call. Shane and Lopez were conducting the interview with Grimes, and she couldn't help but feel a sense of unease. He had not brought an attorney with him. He'd arrived alone, leaving his sister-in-law with the girls at home.

The tension between Shane and Lopez had been palpable during the earlier meeting, and Taylor couldn't help but wonder how that dynamic would play out during the interview.

Hopefully the two of them could keep it together for Grimes' sake.

After what felt like an eternity, the door to the conference room finally swung open, and Sheriff, Shane, and Special Agent Lopez entered. Their expressions were inscrutable, and Taylor couldn't discern the outcome of the interview from their faces.

"Any updates?" Taylor asked, her voice tinged with anticipation.

Sheriff let out a weary sigh as he took a seat at the head of the table. "That's what we're going to discuss together," he replied, motioning for the others to join him.

Lopez and Shane took their seats, and they all formed a somber circle around the conference table. Taylor braced herself for the news about the interview with Grimes.

Shane cleared his throat and began to recount the interview. "We asked Grimes about the events leading up to Lydia's disappearance, and, once again, he provided a detailed account of his days, and hers as he knows it. It all checked out with what we already knew—Lydia was shopping, and he was at work. He even has incidence reports from his shift that make up a tight alibi. We are confident in saying that Grimes was nowhere near Walmart that entire night."

Lopez nodded in agreement. "We also asked him about his relationship with Lydia, and he appeared genuinely distraught about her disappearance. He didn't exhibit any signs of deception during the interview."

Taylor felt a wave of relief wash over her. She had believed in Grimes' innocence, and it was reassuring to hear that their interview had yielded no evidence to suggest otherwise.

Sheriff leaned back in his chair, his expression relieved. "That's good to hear. Now we can focus all our efforts elsewhere."

Lopez interjected, his tone measured and authoritative. "I agree with Sheriff. Barnes and Fisher are our primary suspects, and they're still out there. Hopefully, Lydia is, too. We'll continue to get all their faces out to the media, and work with local law enforcement in North and South Carolina in case they doubled back that way."

Taylor nodded in agreement. "I'd also like to go out and talk to her teenage daughters, Grace and Ella. There might be something they missed telling us. I can do it at their house since they're minors—and friends of mine. I don't want to make them too uncomfortable. Grimes will be there to supervise."

Sheriff gave a nod of approval. "That's a good plan. We need to leave no stone unturned in this investigation."

Lopez took charge, his demeanor confident and focused. "Here's what we'll do next. I'll coordinate with the local authorities in South Carolina and make sure we have a joint task force ready to go as soon as we get word on Barnes and Fisher. Deputy Gray, you go interview the girls, and Shane—"

Shane held a hand up to interrupt Lopez. "Thanks, but I have my own tasks lined up."

Sheriff gave him a warning look. "That might be so but don't try to be a cowboy on this, Weaver. We're working this case as a team. You put everything you're doing up on that board. Do I need to remind you that Special Agent Robbins is lead and Special Agent Lopez must keep him apprised of every move we make?"

Shane nodded as Taylor cringed internally for him. But he didn't seem worried about the verbal slap. Either that or his pride was too strong for him to show his dismay.

As the discussion continued, Taylor was glad that Grimes was officially cleared off the suspect list. She couldn't wait to get over to his house and tell him so, too. At least she could bring him one piece of positive news in the long streak of bad luck he was having.

CHAPTER 10

Cate finished twelve reps without wincing once at the pain in her bicep. She was determined to regain her strength and mobility, and each day brought her closer to that goal. The sun streamed in through the windows, making her melancholy for the days that she could spend all day outside, working her body around the farm. She'd been up since before dawn and had seen Taylor leaving extra early for work. Or at least she'd seen her headlights.

She said a quick prayer for Lydia, and that Taylor and her team would find her today.

Sutton stood in the kitchen, busy preparing a green smoothie.

Cate watched as Sutton expertly blended the ingredients, her movements precise and efficient. It was clear that she was no stranger to the task. Over the last week, they hadn't had any conversation that wasn't just surface level, but Cate was becoming curious about her.

Sutton just didn't give off the criminal vibe. She turned off the blender and approached her with the smoothie in hand.

"Here you go, Cate," Sutton said, offering the glass. "Freshly made with all the good stuff."

Cate accepted the smoothie. "Thank you, Sutton. You're getting the hang of things quickly." She took a drink. "This one tastes better than Anna's, but let's keep that between us."

Sutton chuckled, taking a seat opposite Cate. "Thanks. I added a dash of cinnamon and nutmeg. It helps cover the strong taste of the greens."

Before Cate could respond, the front door of the cabin swung open, and in walked a familiar figure. Jackson, her ex-husband, stood in the doorway, holding a bag from Mabel's.

His hulking presence filled the room with tension. It was weird having him in her personal space.

"Morning," he greeted them. "I brought some breakfast for you both. They're letting you have biscuits again, right?"

Cate sighed inwardly. Ever since the accident, Jackson had been around more than usual, and she was picking up vibes that he wanted to be more than friends and co-grandparents. She was going to have to have another talk with him. The romantic love between them had long since faded. Even if it hadn't, she was done with relationships. She wanted to focus on her health, her daughters and grands, and the work at the farm.

It was enough. And none of it would cause any of the emotional pain that men had caused.

"Thanks, Jackson," she said, trying to keep her tone neutral. "That's kind of you."

Sutton remained quiet, but she got up and went to the kitchen and began washing out the blender.

"And, sorry, but I can't have biscuits yet," Cate said. "Even as good as Mabel makes them, Anna is adamant that I can only put healthy food into my body, at least until after I've fully recovered."

He scoffed, rolling his eyes toward the ceiling. "Anna doesn't have to know. I got you a sausage biscuit, loaded with mayonnaise and lettuce, the way you used to eat them." He glanced at Sutton, but she pretended not to hear.

Cate didn't want to hurt his feelings. But it wasn't about the sausage biscuit. Not totally. She really didn't want to give him false hope that they were going to have a closer relationship.

"Oh, Anna would find out," she said. "But thank you for the thought. Take mine home for your lunch later."

He set the bag on the counter that separated the small kitchen from the living room.

"Okay. No problem. Do you need a ride to rehab today?"

Cate hesitated, her grip on the smoothie glass tightening. She reached for the oxygen tube and put it in, her anxiety making it harder to breathe.

Before she could respond, Sutton spoke up, surprising both Cate and Jackson. "Actually, Cate already has transportation arranged. I'll be taking her to rehab. I have to speak to her therapist today about this week's home exercises."

Jackson's eyebrows shot up in surprise, and he shifted uncomfortably. "Oh, I see. Well, that's good. I guess I'll leave you two to it then."

With a polite nod, he turned to leave, the atmosphere in the cabin heavy with unsaid words and unresolved feelings. He left the bag of biscuits on the counter.

As the door closed behind him, Cate let out a sigh of relief.

"Thank you, Sutton," she said, her voice tinged with gratitude. "I appreciate your help."

Sutton smiled warmly, her calm demeanor a welcome presence amid the awkward encounter. "Of course. I'm here to support you in any way I can. I could tell you weren't feeling it with him."

"We have a long, rocky history," Cate said.

Sutton nodded. "Been there, believe me. Exes are never easy to deal with."

Cate saw pain flash across Sutton's face before she quickly hid it. "Grab a coffee, Sutton, and come sit down for a minute before you head out for chores."

"Okay. Let me pour some coffee first. And I think I will have a biscuit. I'm going to need a lot of energy today, according to what Jo said yesterday. There's a litter of pups coming to the rescue." She puttered around, poured her coffee, and fixed it up with Almond milk from the fridge, then finally sat on the couch, across from Cate.

"How *is* it going out there? You getting used to the bigger dogs yet?" Cate asked.

Sutton put her cup down after taking a long drink. "I think so. Jo showed me the proper way to approach them. Where not to touch them, and some tips about my body language. I'm feeling a little more confident."

"Good," Cate said. "Those are some skills you can take with you and use anywhere. Hart's Ridge is a very dog-friendly town, so you'll never know when you'll be face-to-face with the next doggo."

"Yeah, I've noticed that over the years. It's not just downtown on the square or at the dog park either. I see women bringing their little dogs in Walmart and letting them sit in the shopping carts like kids. The pooches that are wearing clothes and have their hair done up in bows always make me smile."

"Some people in town get angry about the dogs in the stores thing," Cate said. "But they need to consider that it's what happens when you get lonely. The critters take the place of our children, worming their way into our hearts until we start treating them like babies. A lot of our customers who bring in their little dogs for boarding literally go through terrible anxiety when they're away from them. Sometimes it's sad how many times they'll call in to check on them or ask for photos."

"I can imagine."

Cate ran her foot over Brandy's back affectionately. "Good thing Brandy here isn't tiny, or you might see me toting her around in a little leopard purse one day."

"For some reason, I don't see that happening," Sutton said.

"You don't look like the type to dress your dog, nor carry anything leopard. But, yeah, I can see that would be the case with some people. Especially older women who don't have anyone else at home. It gets lonely when you're the only one between those four walls. I miss my girls dearly, but I don't have time for a dog. Probably a good thing!"

"You mentioned an ex. How long have you been divorced?" Cate asked.

Sutton gave a harsh little laugh. "Not long enough."

"I'm sorry. I shouldn't pry." Cate felt the heat fill her face.

Sutton waved off her apology. "It's fine. I grieved our divorce for a long time but now I see I'm better without him."

"Were you married long?"

"Eighteen years. Very long years. It was great the first ten years, but, as the girls grew older, there was just more and more on my shoulders, and I felt like I was raising three children instead of two."

"So, he wasn't a true partner?" Cate asked softly.

"Nope. And it all came to a head one night when we were watching a movie and the main couple looked so happy together. I told him I missed when we were that close."

"He didn't like that statement?"

"First of all, it was the first night in a very long while that I even had time to stop and watch a movie. I had to let a lot go to do it and I was shocked with how my comment set him off. He remarked something about how he misses it too and wishes we had the sex life we had back then."

Cate's gaze remained fixed on Sutton. She encouraged her to continue, silently offering a safe space to unload her feelings.

Sutton's hands trembled slightly as she gestured to herself. "I was calm at first. I asked him how the hell he expected me to want sex when I barely had time to take a shower at night." She paused, her eyes revealing a mixture of anger and sadness. "I felt like, if that's all he's missing in our relationship, we just weren't on the same page anymore."

Cate's heart ached for Sutton, who was bravely sharing her vulnerability. She couldn't help but imagine the emotional turmoil and exhaustion she'd lived with. But then she remembered, Jackson was like that, too.

In their later years all he wanted to do was drink while she held the weight of the world on her shoulders. Cate's memories came flooding back. The long nights waiting up for her husband to come back from the bar. The mornings he slept late, unable to shake off his hangovers. The making money stretch way too far and the creativity she had to use to feed their girls. Then the morning he'd taken the girls fishing, against Cate's advice, and the fire broke out and killed their son.

He should've been there.

Cate felt nausea rise in her throat and she tried to remove the memory of the flames from her mind.

"I had been holding so much in for so long, that it all came out that night," Sutton continued, her voice quivering, "I was also taking care of my mother who, at the time, was dying of cancer. I told him I was physically, mentally, and emotionally exhausted from doing almost everything on my own. Taking care of my mom. Of the girls and him. That I never had any time to do anything for myself."

Cate's expression remained compassionate and understanding as Sutton listed the overwhelming responsibilities she juggled daily. She could sense the immense pressure Sutton felt. "What did he say to that?" she asked when Sutton paused for a breath.

"He remarked that I just had to learn to say no," Sutton said with a touch of bitterness. "So what was I to say no to? My mom's chemotherapy? Her physical therapy? Her upcoming surgery? Her doctor's appointments? Our girls' orthodontist appointments?

Getting them to volleyball practice? School events?" Sutton's voice quivered with each item on the list, emphasizing the enormity of her responsibilities. "On top of all that, I was still doing a full time job at the hospital, plus doing all the housework, cooking, and managing our finances. What exactly was optional there?"

Cate felt a lump in her throat as Sutton described the sheer magnitude of her daily tasks. She marveled at Sutton's strength but couldn't help but be deeply concerned about her well-being.

"Doesn't sound like any of it was, if he wasn't going to help you pick up the slack."

"Not only would he not help me, but he added so much stress to my life. I was being motherflipping Wonder Woman but to him I was invisible," Sutton concluded, her tone a mixture of exhaustion and defiance. "Two months later I decided to drop my biggest drain on resources. I asked him to move out and he did. A few weeks in, I realized I didn't miss him. The divorce was final the next year and I finished getting the girls on the road to college by myself. Officially, this time. My life is still crazy, and I've continued to be the only present parent, dealing with all the girls' stuff. But I did leave the hospital to go to home health care so that I could bend my schedule a bit and be there for my mother easier."

"Is she still fighting cancer?"

Sutton swallowed hard and she lifted her chin proudly. "No. I lost her a few months ago. She put up a gallant fight, but, in the end, it took her."

"But you were beside her and I can tell, you are a force to be reckoned with," Cate said. Her eyes glistened with tears, moved by Sutton's honesty and resilience. She realized that Sutton was not just a guest anymore; she was becoming a friend.

Sutton smiled weakly. "Yeah, tell that to the judge in a few months. I might end up a force behind bars. But at least then I might find the time to shave my legs."

CHAPTER 11

After Taylor left Tractor Supply, and confirmed with video that the manager, John, was there and accounted for the entire day and evening that Lydia was abducted, she headed to the Grimes' house, and pulled her cruiser to a stop in the street. She turned off the motor and sat for a moment, taking some deep breaths as she tried to separate her emotions from the task at hand. It was going to be hard to see Grimes and his girls and witness the pain they were going through. It was much easier to work a case when she did not know those involved.

However, that was part of small-town life.

The house's exterior exuded a sense of warmth and familiarity. She'd been there several times and remembered the welcoming porch and white picket fence that framed the front yard. It was the kind of place where laughter and family gatherings seemed to have left an unforgettable mark. There was a Thanksgiving wreath on the front door, most likely put there by Lydia, who would've had the Halloween stuff taken down the day after the holiday. She was always on top of things like that and probably had Christmas lights up the day after Thanksgiving every year.

As she stepped out of her car and approached the front door, a cat that had been sleeping on the windowsill jumped down and ran off.

Taylor couldn't help but notice other small details that defined their home. A porch swing, slightly weathered but well loved, hung from the eaves. A purple, girls' ten-speed bike was leaned against the porch railing, its worn wheels a testament to the passing of time.

At the door, a mat customized with a mom and dad stick figure, plus three girl figures, and *Welcome to the Grimes House* across it in gold lettering.

She knocked and the door opened quickly, revealing Grimes, his eyes bloodshot and hair a mess. He was dressed in jeans and a sweatshirt, his outdoor shoes on like he was ready to bolt at any time in case he got the call that they'd found Lydia.

"Deputy Grimes," Taylor greeted him with a sympathetic nod.

"Caleb," he corrected her gently, as if the formalities in his own home were too hard to bear.

"Caleb," she repeated with a nod.

"It's been five days, Taylor," he said softly. "Where is she?"

Taylor sighed heavily. "I wish we knew. But I'd like to talk with Ella and Grace. I want to see if I can pry their memories for anything that might help us."

"Believe me, I've tried," he said. "But you're welcome to have a go, too. Come on in."

Upon entering the house, Taylor was met with an atmosphere that was both comforting and chaotic. It was clear that the usual order of the household had been disrupted by Lydia's absence. Toys were scattered across the living room floor, evidence of Ella's and Grace's attempts to keep their baby sister, Zoey, entertained.

The walls were adorned with family photos, capturing moments of joy and togetherness. It was a snapshot of a life that had been abruptly interrupted.

Grace was in the kitchen, and it appeared she was making up bottles of formula.

Ella sat on the couch, holding a restless Zoey in her arms. The room was filled with the soft hum of a baby mobile, its gentle melodies a soothing backdrop to the somber atmosphere. Ella's eyes were red from tears and worry.

"Sorry for the mess," Grimes said. "It's been a lot."

"Please. Don't apologize. That doesn't matter," Taylor said, feeling a pang of sympathy for all of them as she observed the signs of their struggle to maintain a semblance of normalcy.

"Lydia's sister went home to get more clothes and to check on things," he said, then took the baby and sat in the rocking chair. He began to rock and make soothing noises. Seeing him out of uniform and in his role as a loving father made Taylor's fear for Lydia's absence even more palpable.

This was a family.

A family who needed their matriarch.

She chose a spot on the couch, mindful of the scattered toys, and took a deep breath to steady herself. This was going to be a hard interview and she needed to keep her emotions in check.

"Grace, come in here," Grimes said.

She came and sat down beside Ella. Both girls looked terrified and that was to be expected, considering their lives had been overturned.

"Grace. Ella," Taylor began gently, "I know this is incredibly difficult for all of you, but I need to ask you some questions and I want you to think really hard before you answer."

Grace appeared to steel herself and she put her arm around her little sister. "Okay," she replied in a trembling voice.

Her anxiety was profound. Taylor knew that Lydia's absence had taken a toll on the entire family, but especially Grace who had been left to stand in as her mother in helping the most with baby Zoey.

Taylor concentrated on providing a comforting presence

amidst the turmoil. "We are doing everything we possibly can to find your mom, Grace, but can you tell me about that night when she called from the store? What did she say? How did she sound? Could you hear anything in the background?"

"She called my phone, but I put her on speaker so that Ella could hear, too," Grace said. "She was kind of quiet, but she said she was going to be later than expected because she had a few more places to shop. She sounded ... I don't know, normal, I guess. But I couldn't hear anything unusual."

Taylor nodded, absorbing the information. They knew now that the call was made right before the ATM transaction and, most likely, the two men were in the car with her. "Did she mention anything specific? Anyone she was with, or anything that caught her attention?"

Both girls exchanged glances, trying to recall the details of that fateful call.

"No, she just said she was going to be late, and I told her to take her time, that Zoey was fine," Grace said, and her voice broke. She looked down at the floor, hiding her tears. "I wanted her to have some time to enjoy herself for once. She does everything for everyone else and never gets to do anything fun by herself."

"Grace, I've told you," Grimes said. "It's not your fault. Your mom wasn't asking your permission. She'd already made her mind up. She was only telling you."

Grace nodded slowly, but Taylor saw a tear roll off her nose and land on the toe of her pink Converse sneaker. Ella reached over and took her sister's hand, squeezing it.

"And you're sure you couldn't hear anything else? Anything at all?" Taylor said.

Grace shook her head. "No. Nothing."

Taylor looked at Ella. "Ella? What about you?"

Ella closed her eyes, clearly straining to recall every detail. "I ... I think I might've heard a man's voice in the background, but I couldn't make out what he was saying. It was just a brief second. Then later I figured it was probably the radio."

Taylor's heart quickened at the mention of a man's voice. It was a potential lead, something to add to the board. She jotted down the information in her notebook. "Thank you, Ella. That's important."

"Ella, why didn't you tell me that?" Grimes said, suddenly alert and upright in the seat, jolting the baby. "I've asked you both a million times if you heard anyone else on the call."

She squirmed. "I just *said* why, Dad. I thought it was the radio, but now, I'm not sure."

"Jeez, Dad. Chill," Grace said. "You were just about to get Zoey to sleep."

Zoey was thrusting her little fists in the air, looking like she was about to ramp up to a tantrum.

"It's okay, guys," Taylor said, trying to ease the sudden tension. "We'll add it to the report. Might've been the radio. We just don't know."

Ella looked relieved that it wasn't going to become a big deal.

They really didn't give Taylor anything else helpful. It was disappointing, but she'd tried, and now she needed to get back to the department.

Zoey began to wail, and Grimes stood, then began pacing with her. "She's been colicky since Lydia disappeared. I don't know how to calm her down."

"We've tried everything," Grace added.

The three of them looked so stressed. Taylor's heart ached for the baby most of all. Her cries probably had nothing to do with colic.

Zoey wanted her mother. No, she *needed* her mother.

Taylor offered a reassuring smile. "She's picking up on the tense atmosphere and it's making her upset. Babies can sense when something is wrong even if they don't quite understand what. Why don't you let me see what I can do."

Grimes handed her over as though he was relieved to get her out of his arms. He went back to the chair and sat down, his head in his hands.

Taylor took her over to the couch where a small receiving blanket lay wadded in the corner. With one arm she held Zoey, and with the other she smoothed the blanket out flat, noting the tiny, pink elephants all over it.

She placed Zoey right in the middle, then quickly wrapped her up, burrito style. She tucked the corners in as tight as she could, then put Zoey against her shoulder and moved her back and forth while whispering in her ear.

It took about three to four minutes, but finally Zoey settled.

Taylor met Grimes' eyes and he smiled softly, but it didn't reach his sad eyes.

Ella elbowed her sister to look, and they both watched Taylor with the baby.

Another five minutes and Zoey drifted off to sleep.

Grace stood and led the way to the nursery as Taylor snuggled Zoey close to her chest and tried to transfer all the reassurance she could to the tiny girl.

CHAPTER 12

Sutton looked hilariously tiny behind the steering wheel of Cate's van. Her petite legs barely reached the pedals, but she drove it like a boss. She'd offered to use her own car many times, but Cate always refused. It wouldn't be fair to put wear and tear on her car, or use up her gasoline, when it was Cate's appointments that they did all the running to.

They'd just left the surgeon's office and he was pleased with Cate's improvement, but the downside was he wanted her to continue physical therapy for now. He refused to release her to lift over five pounds or to drive a car, so she was all in her feelings about not having her freedom back yet. There was good news, though. No more portable oxygen tank to drag around. She was off that now.

"Want to hear the radio?" Sutton asked, glancing over at her.

"No, not really."

"We could do car karaoke?" she teased.

Cate gave her a half smile. "Believe me, you don't want to hear me sing."

"I promise it would be better than my attempts."

Still, they rode in silence for another five miles before Sutton went off course, toward downtown.

"Where are you going?" Cate asked.

"I'm not taking you back yet. I think we need some R&R. How about lunch out today? My treat."

"What about your afternoon chores?"

Sutton winked at her. "No problem. I talked to Jo before I left. She and Cecil have it covered, and Levi got his name called out at school and is going to be doing all the things he hates to do around the farm for his punishment."

"He loves everything around the farm," Cate said. "And what does that mean, 'got his name called out?'"

She shrugged. "Just that he was probably talking in class or something. Nothing major. And there are a few things he doesn't like to do."

"Like what?"

"Anything to do with the chickens, according to his mom."

Cate laughed. She'd forgotten about that. The entire chicken project was all from Anna. She thought it would be good for the kids and since they were planting a garden next spring, they were going to recycle the manure for fertilizer.

Bronwyn took to the chickens immediately but, for some reason, Teague and Levi just about got their hands pecked off every time they tried to retrieve the eggs.

"Jo said he's going to be on scoop duty as well as have to get eggs," Sutton said.

"I'll make a point to be out there, then. I could use a good laugh."

Sutton turned down a side street.

"You sure could. You look like a walking mood forecast. And today is grumpy with a chance of grouchiness."

"Sorry. I miss my independence."

"I get it," Sutton said. "But you'll get it back soon. You're lucky, Cate. Did you know that last year more than forty-eight thousand people in the United States died of a gunshot? You aren't a statistic, but you almost were. Be patient."

She was right. Cate's patience had worn thin. Everyone wanted to check in on her, make her eat the right things, drink the special concoctions, and check off every single task ever written in the manual for surviving an injury like hers. Her phone had never gone off so much with text messages, memes, and reminders. The girls were showing her that they cared for her, and it made Cate feel like a jerk that it was overwhelming. She probably needed counseling. Her doctor had said as much, but if she got through decades behind bars without it, this should be a cake walk.

"I'll try harder," she finally said.

Sutton pulled into a parking space at the square, shut off the engine, and turned to look Cate full in the face.

"Are you starving?" she asked.

"No." Cate released her seat belt and picked her purse up from the floor.

"Then I have another idea. Instead of sitting down and having a boring lunch and mundane chit chat, why don't we go do something fun?" She looked delighted at her idea.

"Like what?" Cate asked.

"I don't know. What would you like to do?"

"I literally cannot think of a single fun thing that doesn't involve what I already do at the farm. I like my job. It's where I find my comfort. The dogs get me and don't smother me or ask questions," Cate said, smiling slightly.

"Okay—so *animals*." Sutton said, then leaned back against her seat, thinking. Then she opened her eyes wide. "I know just the thing. Put your seatbelt back on."

THE VAN RUMBLED to a stop in front of a mechanical gate, and Cate peered out of the window, curiosity bubbling inside her. They'd gone way out in the country and down a long, dirt road to a dead end.

"Where are we?" she asked, her eyes scanning the surroundings.

Sutton turned to her with a mischievous grin. "You said you prefer animals to humans, so I've brought you to visit another sanctuary. One where you won't have to get all dirty, or obsess about not helping out, and you can just enjoy yourself and let go."

Cate nodded, intrigued by what lay beyond the gate. They stepped out of the van, and a cool breeze rustled through the trees. The entrance was adorned with a colorful sign welcoming them to "The Haven Zoo," and once they pushed a buzzer, the gate opened.

As they entered, a friendly brunette emerged to greet them. "Hey there! I'm Johnnie Sue," she said, her energy infectious. "Welcome to the madhouse."

"I've met you before," Sutton said. "You're the founder and owner, right?"

She nodded. "That's me. Also, the caretaker, transporter, groundskeeper, and everything else under the sun, especially when I can't get enough volunteers."

"Yeah, I brought out some fresh produce a few times last year," Sutton said. "Also, several fruit baskets that were sent to my mother. In her final days she couldn't eat much of anything, but people kept bringing it."

"Oh, yes. I remember now. Thank you for that," Johnnie Sue said. "We have a few weekly donors who are angels to remember us. But we always appreciate the in-betweeners. There's always a shortage of fresh food for the animals. I keep a stockpile of canned fruits and veggies for the hard weeks."

Cate was excited to see what animals were on the property.

She extended her hand with a smile. "Nice to meet you, Johnnie Sue. This place looks amazing. I didn't even know it was here."

"Well, this is one of the only zoos in Georgia that cares for rhesus macaque monkeys. We also have the only African serval. As well as lemurs, horses, goats, llamas, a donkey, pigs, chickens, and peacocks. Cats from the local shelter even have a place and a job here, and we have two Great Pyrenees rescues, Mollie and Maya, guarding the perimeter."

Johnnie Sue beamed with pride as she led them down the driveway. To their right was a fenced-in area with a few outbuildings, and various animals roaming within.

Behind that was a humble modular home with a small porch.

To the left, Cate could see two fenced-in areas. One was occupied by a donkey and in the other were several enclosures, with a small path that walked between them.

It didn't look like any zoo that Cate had ever seen. There was nothing fancy or high tech and you could tell that most of the upkeep was done by a minimal amount of people, but it appeared to be lovingly cared for.

The two huge, white dogs bounded over and Sutton stepped behind Cate, until Johnnie Sue laughed and said they would never hurt her.

She came out and offered her hand—palm up, as Jo had instructed—for them to sniff. One of them wagged its tail enthusiastically, and the other backed away, barking defensively. Cate laughed as Sutton jumped behind her again. She obviously needed more experience with the big dogs.

The bigger one barked again, deep and throaty. Cate could see how they'd easily scare off intruders in the night, by their bark alone.

"Oh, stop," Johnnie Sue waved them off, affectionately. "They think they're the boss, but, I tell you, they're fantastic to have around here at night when the coyotes start yipping. They won't let anything happen on their watch."

She led them to a special enclosure and introduced them to the zoo's longest-term resident. "Meet Zachary," she said, pointing to a rhesus macaque monkey. "He's been here for ages. We've celebrated two decades of birthdays for him. Don't get too close though. He can be ornery."

Cate's heart warmed at the sight of the wise-looking monkey. He watched them suspiciously, his eyes following every step they made.

It was obvious how much Johnnie Sue loved the animals by the way she talked about how they were rescued and came to be a part of her family. The enclosures were secure and outfitted with different swings and toys, even little riding ones that toddlers used. Each arena included a small area for the monkeys to get out of the cold, with blankets and heaters. There were buckets fixed to the outside of the pens, some showing remains of the fruit that was placed there earlier.

Johnnie Sue continued, "We've also had four lemur rescues. Mason just turned one and joined our adult lemurs, Dax and Jax. The babies, Tag, Rachel, and Joey, required a lot of care initially, but they're growing and thriving now."

While they were standing close to Zachary's enclosure, the mischievous old monkey reached out through the wire and snatched Cate's phone from her hand. With a triumphant screech, he ran off, holding it like a prized possession.

"Oh, no. That's why I said don't get too close," Johnnie Sue said. Then she scolded the monkey. "Give it back, Zach. Throw it to me!"

Cate and Sutton burst into laughter as Zachary began taking selfies, then turned and snapped pictures of them, thoroughly amusing himself.

"Oh, Zachary, you rascal!" Cate chuckled. She hoped he wouldn't break her phone, but, if he did, it was her own fault.

Johnnie Sue changed tactics and tried to coax the cheeky monkey into giving the phone back, but Zachary was having too much fun. "Come on, Zachary, be a good monkey and give it back," she said, her voice pleading. "I'll give you extra treats tomorrow if you do."

Zachary hooted and showed no signs of returning the phone. He ran around the enclosure, holding it high above his head, hopping or swinging from stand to stand at a dizzying pace.

Cate gave it a try. "Hey there, buddy! Can I have my phone back, please?"

But Zachary was in no mood to comply. He suddenly tossed the phone high into the air where it went sailing out of a hole in metal fencing, and it landed in an adjacent monkey enclosure.

Another monkey grabbed the phone and scurried up a tree.

"Oh, great. Now Dax and Jax are going to play keep away," Johnnie Sue said.

Sutton laughed heartily and turned to Johnnie Sue. "Looks like we've got ourselves a monkey photo shoot! Do they have a good sense of composition?"

Johnnie Sue chuckled. "With all this practice, they're definitely improving their skills!"

As they approached, Jax wrestled the phone away from Dax and tossed it to another enclosure where a tiny monkey got her tiny hands on it.

"Rachel," scolded Johnnie Sue.

Rachel cackled with glee and began taking pictures of Joey, who appeared to be somewhat of a class clown as he mimicked humans with silly poses, sending everyone into fits of laughter.

Cate found an untouched apple and approached the pen. "Come on, guys, this apple's a fair deal, right? Look how delicious it is."

The monkeys chattered among themselves, seemingly considering her offer. After a moment, Rachel scurried over and accepted the apple, then handed the phone back to Cate, victorious.

"Thank you, dear," Cate said, completely enamored.

It was worth risking her phone for the show they'd put on.

But Zachary, the original culprit, threw a tantrum because the other monkeys had ruined his game. He bellowed and crossed his arms over his chest, glaring at them furiously. He reminded Cate of a pot-bellied little man with scrawny legs.

They couldn't help but laugh at his sudden scowl.

With the phone safely back in Cate's hands, they continued their tour, meeting various animals, including pigs who feasted on leftover Halloween pumpkins, Caroline the llama, and a three-legged llama named Dash.

Rocky, the donkey, greeted them with a friendly bray, and Asante, the African serval cat, observed their every move with sleek and quiet curiosity. Johnnie Sue said the cat came to her when its owner was caught with it in a state where it was illegal to have as a pet.

Cate couldn't imagine why any states allowed the gorgeous but wild-looking cats to be kept as household pets. Asante looked like he should be in a jungle somewhere, stalking his dinner, but someone raising him as a domestic animal had taken that opportunity away from him.

"Johnnie Sue once met Jane Goodall," Sutton said. "I almost forgot about that."

Johnnie Sue nodded humbly. "Sure did. It's one of the highlights of my life. Happened many years ago at Georgia State."

"Did you go to school there?" Cate asked, curious as to how she'd gotten involved in wildlife. She also wondered if she was married or had children but wouldn't dare ask.

"Yep. Got my Masters in anthropology. I was awarded an international affiliation with Brazil to complete my undergrad and do my thesis research on human and primate interactions in Rio de Janeiro."

As the tour wound down, Johnnie Sue introduced them to a lively group of chickens, roosters, and two ducks named Beauty and Beast, who had survived a vicious coyote attack in which others in their flock were decimated and eaten.

Johnnie Sue shared her struggles to care for the rescues, mentioning ongoing needs of everything from fruit bars and canned veggies to heating lamps and beds. How she managed everything she did was quite amazing.

Cate admired Johnnie Sue's dedication and the love she poured into the zoo. She hoped that one day she'd be able to create a legacy to be proud of, just as Johnnie Sue obviously had.

CHAPTER 13

Cate was still smiling when they left the zoo and were miles away. The tour had filled her with such joy, and she hoped that in the future they could help Johnnie Sue out with some needs. Cate knew from experience how hard it was to get regular donations.

Sutton picked up on her fatigue and, instead of going to a restaurant as she'd said they would, she whipped into the drive-through at McDonald's and ordered burgers, fries, and two large sweet teas.

Cate's eyes widened in shock and Sutton turned to her after paying.

"Today you get a break from your healthy diet. We won't tell Anna," she said, winking.

"She would hang you by your toenails if she knew," Cate said, laughing as she visualized Anna blowing her stack over the crap Cate was about to put into her body. But her appetite was suddenly stirred. She wasn't much for fast food, but, when you aren't allowed something, that's when you decide you want it, and she couldn't wait to devour some salty French fries.

"Want to eat in the parking lot?" Sutton asked when they pulled away.

"What about the lake landing?" Cate said. "It's only a few miles from here and we can watch the water while we eat."

Sutton approved, and five minutes later they were parked with a front row seat to the view. It was chilly so they stayed in the van with the windows slightly open to let out the McDonald's aroma and allow some fresh air in.

Cate watched the ducks gliding gracefully across the lake. It looked so peaceful and was soothing to her busy thoughts. "We need a pond. And ducks. Beauty and Beast were cute."

"Cute, yes, but ducks are pooping machines," Sutton said. "Better watch what you wish for. They'll be up on your porches and in the driveway, leaving calling cards all over the place."

She had a point. Cate would keep the duck idea to herself for a while.

They unwrapped their sandwiches and began to eat, quiet while the gentle breeze rustled the leaves of nearby trees.

"Mmm ..." Cate said. "I'm not usually a McDonald's fan but sometimes it just hits the spot."

"Got that right," Sutton said, her mouth full as she grinned. After a few bites, she looked at Cate, her expression thoughtful.

Cate noticed the contemplative look on Sutton's face and smiled. "You look like you've got something on your mind. Spill it."

Sutton hesitated for a moment, then decided to ask her a question. "I hope this doesn't offend you, Cate, but I've been curious. What was it like in prison?"

Cate paused, her gaze turning distant for a moment as she remembered her time behind bars. She didn't like to talk about it. Hell, she didn't even like to think about it, though for some reason she still couldn't release those memories. She still felt like a prisoner at times. In the dead of the night sometimes she felt like if she opened her eyes, she'd find herself staring up at the metal bottom of the bunk bed above her.

It had brought chills to her arms, it felt so real.

The fact that Sutton knew about her past was unsettling. As though she'd been stripped naked and paraded before her.

"How do you know about that?" she asked, struggling to keep her voice even.

"Are you angry? I'm sorry, Cate. Really, just forget it." Sutton nervously fumbled with her sandwich wrapper, looking anywhere but at Cate.

"Stop fiddling. I need to know. Who told you?"

Sutton turned to her and grimaced. "Well," she began, "my daughter used to date a volunteer fireman's son in town, and he heard about your story from his dad, who heard it from the chief."

Small town grapevine.

Cate didn't even know any of the firemen. Nor the chief. But something told her she needed to find a way to talk to him and keep his mouth shut about her business. But that wasn't Sutton's fault.

She took a deep breath and decided to answer the question.

"What sucks most about prison," she began, "is leaving your family and not being there for the important things. When one of your kids gets hurt or sick, and, God forbid, when someone you love dies and you can't be there. It's the most helpless feeling in the world and for me that's the worst part about prison."

Sutton's face had gone pale. She was probably thinking about not being able to see her girls. A mother's biggest nightmare was being separated from children who needed her.

Cate continued. "Next is the poor healthcare. I had an ear infection for nearly four years one time because they wouldn't prescribe the correct antibiotics."

"Isn't that against the law to deny you medical care?"

"Lots of things they do to you in prison are against the law. You're a number and nothing more."

Sutton listened intently, her curiosity appearing genuine.

"Everything else is what you make of it," Cate continued. "I made friends there who are more loyal and real than the people I grew up around. Prison is the great equalizer. It doesn't matter where you came from or how much money you have. When you get there, you all wear the same color, eat the same food, and live in the same place. That's when you find out what people are really made of underneath their polished lives."

"Were you bored out of your mind?" Sutton asked. "I hate being bored."

Cate paused, her eyes meeting Sutton's. "Sometimes, but I chose to stay as busy as I possibly could. I took the opportunity to sign up for a lot of things. Like dog training and horticulture. I helped other inmates in their drug programs, teaching them that their addictions led them to incarceration, and they must be accountable for their choices. Together we learned to incorporate gratitude and humility every day, and to think about what our own core values were going to be when released."

"I've been reading a lot about corruption in prisons," Sutton said.

Cate took a moment to sip her tea before continuing. "Yeah, state prisons are corrupt, as well as privatized prisons. It's a well-oiled machine that struggles to do what they were meant to do. Rehabilitate. Especially because your physical needs are barely met, so of course your emotional needs are going to be ignored by those who run the prisons, and then you are just doing what you can to survive your time."

She looked out at the peaceful lake for a moment, collecting her thoughts. "To them, you become part of a herd, like cattle, wearing your inmate number like a cow with a brand. Thieves are everywhere, too. Nothing is safe. What the thieves don't take, the guards—" she suddenly realized what she'd said.

"I'm sorry, Sutton. I didn't mean—"

Sutton stopped her. "It's fine. I didn't take offense. Please, keep going. I want to know all I can."

Cate let out her breath. The last thing she wanted to do was hurt someone's feelings.

"Anyway, despite the challenging circumstances, most women in prison tend to be supportive of each other. It's like we become a family in there. After a few years of watching the new arrivals struggle during intake, I began helping them those first days when everything is terrifying and new. Half the time the prison didn't give them their basic needs when they got there, and they were expected to wait until someone put money on their books to buy it from the commissary themselves. And many of them didn't have anyone on the outside to put money in. I collected toiletry packs, coffee, and cigarettes from more prosperous inmates, and, when new inmates arrived and didn't have what they needed, I'd go to them and offer what I could to help ease their transition."

Sutton smiled, obviously touched by the resilience and creativity of the women in prison.

"It sounds like you were a source of support and comfort for many during your time there. It's incredible how the women looked out for each other."

"Don't get me wrong," Cate said. "It's no walk in the park. There's also plenty of drama, gossip, and the relationships—Lord, help! Their love lives caused all sorts of trouble. There's violence, too, and you must always be on guard. It's all up to you to not get caught up in the bad stuff. Do your time quietly and keep your nose clean."

"Did you get caught up?"

Cate shook her head. "Never. I wasn't supposed to be there anyway and had no plans to make my life worse than it was. I did have close friends though. It helps to find people you can trust. Those in my cellblock did things as a family living together would. We ate together. Went out to the yard together. Tried to get work assignments together. We even had a strict schedule to keep our cellblock clean, and showers were scrubbed every day. When someone was having a heavier monthly than normal, and needed more than the very few sanitary napkins they were allotted each month from supplies, others pitched in to make sure everyone stayed clean and kept their dignity."

"You're making it sound less scary than I've made it out to be in my head," Sutton said.

"No—don't think like that. I can't tell you what the Georgia prisons are like. They might be totally different and even mine was a very scary place to be. But if you go in with a positive attitude, you'll find ways to not lose your mind. Some of the inmates in my block used their creative skills to decorate for the holidays and birthdays, too. Ever seen a cake made with honey buns, cookies, and all other sorts of snack items thrown in a bag, then ironed out?"

Sutton laughed. "Can't say that I have. Luckily, I don't have much of a sweet tooth. Other than this southern tea, I mean."

"You still might find yourself buying sweets," Cate said, chuckling. "You wouldn't believe what people will trade for a honey bun or two."

"Well, I guess we should be getting back before your daughter, the warden, starts calling to find out where we are," Sutton teased.

"Wait," Cate said. "Before we go, I have a question for you."

"Shoot."

"Do you really think you'll be going to jail? Want to talk about it?"

Sutton hesitated, then put the car in reverse. "Give me another day or so, and then I might tell you all about it."

Cate nodded and looked out the window.

Trust was a funny thing. It was the hardest thing in the world to gain, and easiest to lose. She ought to know—trust was something she felt very little of anymore. Other than her girls, everyone else in her life had let her down. Her parents. Jackson. The justice system. And now Ellis. She didn't blame Sutton one bit for keeping her guard up.

"But thanks for asking. I appreciate you," Sutton added softly, then turned on the radio.

CHAPTER 14

Two more days passed, and Taylor, Shane, and the agents processed leads and discarded them just as fast, then they hit on a real one. Taylor had finally just fallen asleep after chugging NyQuil when the text came through.

> Get to the department. Stat.

In the bathroom she pulled her hair back into the tight bun she'd worn all day before coming home, and she splashed her face with cold water before going to her closet and finding jeans and a sweatshirt and slipping on her casual holster belt.

She was not getting back into her uniform. Not in the middle of the night and not when she was so sleepy she could barely function.

Diesel padded in behind her and yawned, then did a downward dog pose. When he straightened again, he gave her a perplexed look.

"I know, boy. Go back to sleep." She wished he could go with her. The sheriff had put a stop to him riding along or coming to the department when Dottie began bringing her tiny Chihuahua to work and claiming she thought suddenly that all dogs were allowed.

Taylor and Sam passed him back and forth between their homes, but when she was working a lot of hours she missed him desperately. She wondered what he thought of the joint custody situation, and if he missed her, too.

She glanced quietly at her bed as she opened the small gun safe and took out her piece, then carefully slipped it into her side holster.

Sam lay there, completely knocked out with his arms over his head.

She hoped she could get out of the room, then the cabin, without waking either him or Alice.

To be precise, it was two thirty in the morning. Taylor had spent the two previous hours going back through the old profiles of the two women Barnes and Fisher had left behind in Georgetown, looking for anything that could be valuable. Shared friends. Where they'd taken their vacations. Favorite spots to visit. Then she'd moved on to family members of the men. Brothers. Sisters. Mom and Dad. A third cousin twice removed, or, hell, even five times removed.

Just someone with a connection. Anyone.

There had to be a clue as to where the men had gone to hide out with Lydia.

She tiptoed through the kitchen and grabbed her wallet and keys, then crept past Alice on the couch. She looked so content there, as if she belonged. Taylor still couldn't get over the surprise that had met her when she'd finally returned home to what she thought would be an empty house, but instead held her two favorite humans, her best dog, and pizza.

The pizza was cold, but it was the thought that counted. Alice said they'd tried to wait for her, but considering Taylor hadn't gotten away from the department until ten o'clock, it was long past supper time and they'd finally eaten.

Diesel whined and she turned and quietly shushed him, then let herself out the door.

As she climbed into her truck, she checked her surroundings, making sure everything looked right. Since Eldon had broken their trust and gone after her family, Taylor still didn't feel completely safe. It was going to take a while.

Quickly, but quietly, she drove past Cate's dark cabin, then Jo's, Cecil's, and finally the house where Anna and the kids were. Nothing looked out of place, so she headed to the gate and hit the button clipped to her visor, then drove out.

Only a few miles down the road, a deer with a six-point rack jumped into the highway and stood frozen, looking into the headlights of her truck.

Suicidal much?

She lay on the horn, and the animal took off, leaping gracefully out of her way, but she drove slowly for the next mile in case it had others with it who also harbored a death wish. On the roadside, she spotted an armadillo doing a little jig as it searched for snacks.

Town was deathly quiet, too. A good thing considering their manpower during the witching hours was a bare minimum. She was so wrapped up in Lydia's case that she had no idea who was on duty. Usually, she kept up with the schedule in her head.

She drove by a man on a moped. He was hunched over the handlebars to protect himself from the cold wind, but at least he wore an orange vest so he could be seen. As she went around, he waved at her, and she recognized him from court. He'd lost his license due to driving while intoxicated. His mother had tried to persuade the judge to have pity on him.

The judge had promptly told her that he had no pity for a man of forty years old who was stupid enough to jeopardize others with a deadly weapon and then bring his elderly mother to court to beg for his pardon. He then went on to tell her it was long past time to stop enabling him before he ended up killing himself or someone else.

Taylor wondered where he was going at this time of night. If she wasn't in such a hurry, she'd have stopped and asked him.

That reminded her, she should be on patrol rotation with the others. They were taking up her slack and she didn't know how long her peers were going to put up with her being pulled off to be Shane's unofficial partner in detective work.

They were bound to start feeling a certain way over it, but, as long as the sheriff was the one putting her in the role, then they couldn't say much.

When she pulled into the department, among the handful of vehicles, she recognized those belonging to Shane, Lopez, and the sheriff.

To get Sheriff Dawkins out of bed at this hour, it had to be important.

She parked and quickly made her way inside and to the conference room. When she opened the door, Lopez was at the board, writing.

The sheriff and Shane were at the table taking notes.

They all looked her way.

"What's going on?" Taylor asked.

"We know where Barnes and Fisher were two days after leaving Georgetown, South Carolina," Lopez said.

"Where?"

"Augusta, Georgia. Four hours from here," Shane said.

"What were they doing?" Taylor asked warily.

"What they do best," Shane said. "Criminal activity."

Lopez picked it up, leaving out the sarcasm. "On November thirteenth, two men called the authorities to report a home invasion. Barnes and Fisher broke into the home of Simon Jenkins, unaware that he was upstairs sleeping. As they were snooping around and gathering up firearms to steal, Jenkins crept downstairs and confronted them. Fisher and Barnes were attempting to leave just as Simon Jenkins' father was pulling up. Fisher was already in the car and attempted to ram Jenkins Sr.'s car but stopped short. Barnes exited the house and began firing, hitting a nearby greenhouse, and shattering the back window of Jenkins Sr.'s car. Jenkins fled the area with Fisher and Barnes in pursuit, still firing."

Taylor sunk into a chair at the table.

Barnes and Fisher were insane.

"Eventually, Fisher and Barnes ceased the chase, and both Jenkins were left unharmed," Sheriff said. "Based on the descriptions of the men and the van, local officials were able to positively ID that it was them."

"But now they have more firearms?" Taylor asked.

Lopez nodded. "They left most of them behind in their hurry, but they were able to grab a few of Jenkins' pistols."

"Now what?"

"Now every uniform from a hundred miles has been looking for the van, but obviously at some point between the thirteenth and the fifteenth they dumped it. That's why they carjacked Lydia. They needed new wheels."

"They have to know they'll never get away," Taylor said.

"Agree," said Shane. "But I don't think they care. Their goal is to wreak as much havoc as they can before they're taken down."

Taylor thought about her visit to the Grimes' home. Grace and Ella, so scared. Caleb, worried out of his mind, and little baby Zoey, not even aware that she may never see her mother again. She tried to shake off the memory. She had to keep her head in the game.

"They would've dumped the van long before coming here," she said. "They know it's on everyone's list to find. So, I'm betting they stole another vehicle right after the shootout. I'll get started pulling up all the stolen car reports between Augusta and here during November thirteenth and the fifteenth. We have to know where they were in case it's a place they took Lydia back to when they grabbed her."

"That's exactly why I called you in," Sheriff said. "We've all got our tasks now. Let's get to work."

He got up and started to walk out of the room, but Lopez's phone rang, and he answered it immediately.

"Yes, sir?" he said, turning away from them.

The Sheriff paused.

Lopez turned away, then suddenly hit the wall with a closed fist, leaving a deep crack in the plaster. For someone as professional as he was to lose his cool that way, they were all shocked into silence, waiting to hear what happened.

"Yes, sir. Yes, sir." Then he hung up and turned back to them.

"We believe there's another female victim. The women talked some more, and they've got details."

Taylor shook her head. It amazed her how two men stupid enough to get thrown in jail were suddenly smart enough to outrun several law enforcement agencies.

CHAPTER 15

Late November in Columbia, South Carolina, was much warmer than in Hart's Ridge. Taylor felt a bead of sweat forming on her brow as they arrived at the local jail. She drove and was accompanied by Shane and Lopez. The sheriff rarely left Hart County, feeling that someone needed to stay behind to oversee any major emergencies.

Taylor wished he had come along though, considering that the tension in the car was thick the entire way. They were all tired, none of them having gone home for sleep since they'd met up in the middle of the night, but Taylor had hoped that the animosity between Shane and Lopez would subside. Instead, it seemed to have intensified. Shane had sat in the backseat on the way up, and, every so often—when Lopez was talking—she could see him make fed up expressions in her side mirror.

The detention center was made up of several sprawling, gray buildings, and the parking lot was full. When they entered the building, Taylor noticed the stark contrast between the austere surroundings of the facility and the warm weather outside. As they checked in, then were escorted to where Robbins waited, the long, dimly-lit corridors seemed to stretch endlessly.

The air was heavy with the scent of disinfectant and the distant echoes of conversations and clinking cell doors.

Special Agent Robbins greeted them in the small conference room within the jail facility. He sat at the head of the table and leaned forward; his eyes focused on the folder in front of him. Niceties were kept to mere seconds.

"Listen up," he began, his voice firm. "During the early morning hours of November eleventh, a local fire department responded to a reported explosion and fire at a rural area twelve miles outside of Georgetown. The responding firemen found a car burning at an old cemetery. It's been identified as belonging to nineteen-year-old Serenity Bond, who has been reported missing."

Taylor exchanged a concerned glance with her colleagues. This was a significant development.

"According to Simpson and Riker," Robbins continued, "later that day, Fisher and Barnes had returned to the hotel carrying muddy clothing, and Fisher indicated that they had stolen some money. They went to breakfast, and Riker and Simpson reported seeing mud, as well as a candy box, in the van. In addition, Barnes was wearing a heart-shaped ring on a necklace around his neck. Barnes told the women that he had stolen the candy from a girl selling it and that he had stolen the ring from a car. Riker also found Bond's photo ID discarded in the van but didn't say anything about it to the men because she was scared. Later that morning, the two men left and never returned."

Taylor felt a sense of urgency wash over her. The burning car and the muddy clothing were crucial pieces of information. She nodded, her mind already formulating questions for the upcoming interviews.

Robbins looked at Shane and Taylor. "Bond's mother told us that her daughter was wearing a heart-shaped ring on a necklace."

"Oh, my God," Taylor said. She instantly thought of Grace Grimes, only sixteen but so close to nineteen.

Those poor parents.

He continued. "Weaver, you'll be with me to interview Simpson. Gray, Lopez, you're taking Riker. Keep your questions focused and to the point. We need any information they can provide about Barnes, Fisher, and, most importantly, Serenity Bond. Remember, they know nothing about Lydia Grimes but anything they do know can possibly help in the search for her, too. Let's get this done."

With their instructions clear, they proceeded to the interviews, determined to uncover any leads that might bring them closer to finding Lydia Grimes.

The interview room was small and utilitarian, with a table and chairs at its center. Harsh fluorescent lighting cast unforgiving shadows on the off-white walls. Taylor and Lopez took their seats, glancing at the heavy steel door as they waited for their interviewee.

Moments later, Annette Riker was escorted into the room by a uniformed officer. Her disheveled appearance and weary eyes spoke of fear and desperation. Her clothing was rumpled, and her mousy-brown hair hung in unkempt strands around her face. She wore handcuffs, a stark reminder of her current predicament.

Taylor couldn't help but feel a sense of sympathy as she watched Riker take a seat across from them. The woman looked lost and broken, far removed from the reckless decisions she had made while on the run with Barnes and Fisher.

Lopez initiated the interview, his tone firm yet not unkind. "Ms. Riker, we understand that you've been through a lot, and we appreciate your cooperation. We're here to gather information about the events leading up to Serenity Bond's disappearance. Can you tell us everything you know?"

"I wish I had never met Billy," Riker said. "I knew he was trouble, but somehow Trixie convinced me they were alright." Her eyes darted between Taylor and Lopez, her expression a mixture of fear and resignation. She began to recount the events of the past few days, just as Robbins had reported. She explained the stolen firearms, the ring, and the stolen checks, but swore the men never mentioned doing anything to the girl.

Taylor listened intently, hoping that somewhere in Riker's story there might be a clue that would lead them to Lydia, too.

Lopez was good, and Taylor took note of his interviewing skills. He was in his position for a reason, and she wasn't going to waste any of her time with him by not paying attention to his methods. A detective role was on her radar, but maybe someday she could dream even bigger.

Riker didn't add anything that Robbins hadn't already told them, but, as the interview progressed, her demeanor shifted from guarded to remorseful. Tears welled up in her eyes as she revealed the extent of her involvement with Barnes and Fisher. "I never meant for any of this to happen," she said, her voice quivering. "I haven't done anything like this before. It was all because of those two. My life is ruined for a few days of what I thought was simply reckless fun. An adventure."

"Did either of them mention any family members? Areas they might be hiding out?" Taylor asked.

"No," Riker said. "They didn't talk about stuff like that. Other than Avery's brother. Avery and Trixie went to see him because he had drugs. Maybe Trixie knows more about him and their family, but I don't. Billy was very close-mouthed and barely talked."

They finally wrapped it up and Riker asked if she could have a bag of potato chips and a soft drink, explaining that no one in her family had stepped up to add money to her books and that she was hungry.

"I don't even have soap or shampoo," Riker said, whining pitifully. "I smell awful."

Lopez declined but Taylor couldn't just leave her that way. The woman had made mistakes—big ones—but she was still human.

"I'll put some money on your books on my way out," Taylor said.

Riker's eyes filled with tears, and she thanked Taylor profusely as the jailer led her away.

AFTER THE INTERVIEWS, Taylor did what she promised and put twenty-five bucks on Riker's books. Then she, along with Shane, Lopez, and Robbins, left the detention center and made their way to the rural cemetery outside of Georgetown.

The drive was somber, the weight of their mission and frustration at not being able to close the case hanging heavy in the air. Trixie Simpson hadn't had much to add that was any different than what her friend had said, according to Shane.

Fisher and his brother came from a dysfunctional family, which was no surprise, and Trixie said the brother looked as screwed up as Fisher. They'd talked about their childhood a bit when they'd gotten high together, and she remembered them discussing how their mother always fought with their father in front of them. That both parents were drunks.

That tidbit didn't move any sympathy from Taylor.

She also came from a dysfunctional family. Fighting. Her father's drinking. Losing her mother at a young age. Her brother had died tragically in a fire. She'd grown up with next to nothing and was expected to take care of her little sisters with it.

But she hadn't turned to crime and drugs. Everyone had a story, and everyone had an opportunity to change the trajectory of their life.

Was it easy? *No.*

But it could be done. She held no pity for those who were too weak to do it.

The cemetery was old and nestled among towering oak trees, their gnarled branches casting eerie shadows on the graves below. As they approached, they could see the remnants of the burned-out car, still smoldering and emitting thin streams of smoke into the crisp November air. The scene was haunting, and Taylor couldn't help a shiver from running up her spine.

Special Agent Robbins took the lead, walking toward the car with purpose. "Serenity Bond was last seen at the mall," he began, his voice solemn. "She had met up with her grandmother to pick out some clothes for her young niece. They parked in different locations, and, after they finished shopping, they went their separate ways. Serenity was never seen again."

Taylor listened intently, her eyes scanning the charred remains of the vehicle. She imagined the young woman going about her day, unaware of the tragedy that would befall her.

"Video footage?" Shane asked.

"Nope. The security system at that mall is outdated and hasn't worked in years. No footage and no witnesses. It's an older shopping center and doesn't get a lot of business. I don't know how they keep the lights on." Robbins continued, "Serenity also sold candy to help pay for her college books. She had a dragonfly crystal hanging from her rearview mirror, and we found this in the wreckage." He held up a small, blackened fragment of what was once a delicate crystal.

Taylor and the others gathered around to examine the shard. It was a poignant reminder of the vibrant life that, hopefully, hadn't been abruptly cut short, but it wasn't looking positive considering the men returned to the motel room without Serenity or any mention of her.

They spread out and walked the rest of the cemetery, searching for any additional clues but found nothing else of significance.

As they prepared to leave, Taylor couldn't shake the sick feeling that had settled over her. Serenity's story might turn out to be the ultimate tragedy, and it served as a reminder of the darkness that could lurk in unexpected places. A girl shopping with her grandmother and then, hours later, gone.

Robbins stood at his car. "I want all of you back in Hart County, following up on anything and everything to find Lydia Grimes. I've assembled a team here that will continue to look for Serenity Bond. They're also setting up for another press conference later today so let's go. We need to get these monsters off the street."

He got in his car and slammed the door.

"I'll drive back," Shane said, but he gestured for Taylor to take the passenger front seat.

She ignored him, letting Lopez have the honor of listening to Shane all the way home. Maybe it would help them get over their childish rivalry.

CHAPTER 16

The next day they were back on the road again after a new lead came through on the FBI tip line, and then was confirmed by the local sheriff's department in Covington, Georgia. Taylor, Shane, and Special Agent Lopez navigated the highway, leaving Hart's Ridge behind and heading toward a small town that had gained notoriety as the filming location for the famous TV series, *Dukes of Hazzard*. Taylor couldn't help but find it ironic that the men had left the most recent tracks in a place known for fictional car chases and hijinks.

As they got closer, Shane broke the silence, his voice tinged with a hint of sarcasm. "Well, ain't this a picturesque place for a showdown with a couple of fugitives? Maybe they'll try to jump a creek in the General Lee."

Lopez chuckled, clearly enjoying the reference to the iconic TV show. "I doubt they're aiming for a stunt show, but you never know."

Taylor couldn't help but smile at the exchange. Maybe the two men were finally laying down their swords. Not a minute too early, as she was tired of the ongoing friction.

Their destination was a small blueberry farm on the outskirts of Covington. The modern farmhouse and barn stood amidst rows of blueberry bushes, their branches empty of the fruit for the winter. Police cars and local authorities were already on the scene, creating an active atmosphere.

A middle-aged woman, who didn't fit the stereotypical image of a farmer's wife, greeted them at the door. Her name was Sarah Gamble, and she and her husband, Leroy, ran the farm with their three teenage sons and a younger daughter. Her agitation was palpable as she recounted the events that had led them to call the FBI tip line.

"We don't use the truck all the time but, when Leroy finally noticed it gone yesterday," she explained, "we played back the security video, and I recognized those men from the press conference the FBI put out. I knew I had to call it in."

They followed Sarah and Leroy into the office, where she played back the surveillance footage on her computer. Taylor confirmed what they all suspected—the two men caught on camera hot-wiring the old farm truck were none other than Fisher and Barnes.

"What's the date on this?" Taylor asked.

"November fourteenth," the woman said.

That was the day before they'd hijacked Lydia. They hadn't kept the truck long then. It had possibly broken down.

"Come on, I'll show you where the truck was sitting," Leroy said.

They proceeded to the barn, where police tape cordoned off the area and officials milled around, examining the scene. Lopez took photographs of footprints in the muddy ground leading up to the barn's entrance—two distinct sets of prints stood out as different than those of Leroy's, evidence that it was a two-man job.

Taylor listened as Sarah described the stolen vehicle. "It's a 2000 Ford Ranger," she said. "Not worth much, but it's been a reliable workhorse for us. Leroy used it for the farm, and it's always dependable."

There went Taylor's theory on why the men hijacked Lydia.

Shane leaned in, his detective instincts kicking into gear. "Any distinct features or modifications on the truck? Anything that could help us identify it more easily?"

Sarah nodded; her brow furrowed in concentration. "There's a dent on the passenger side, near the rear wheel well. Leroy hit a tree a while back, and we never got around to fixing it. Other than that, it's a pretty standard old farm truck."

"Just so you know," Taylor said. "We're fairly sure they dumped your truck. You probably saw where they are the prime suspects in a carjacking in Hart County. They wouldn't have grabbed that one if they were still in your truck, but it's still important to find so we can see where they were when they dumped it."

"Understandable," Sarah said. "I did see about that woman. So sad. I hope you find her."

"We understand the focus is on finding that lady, but we also have our family to think about. We have children and I don't want those men anywhere near here again," Leroy said. "Do you think we could have someone out here for a few days, in case they come back?"

"I assure you, Mr. Gamble," Lopez said. "They aren't coming back. They're running as far and as hard as they can, but I'll see what I can do to get some coverage out here for a few more nights."

"Thank you, sir," Leroy said. "We're well armed. I just don't want no one sneaking up on us in the middle of the night."

The drive back was somber.

"They'll find that truck burned out somewhere," Taylor said.

No one replied.

Lopez was infuriated that the men were staying a few steps ahead of them. Shane was busy on his laptop, hooked to a hotspot as they went so that he could continue to monitor incoming tips, and Taylor couldn't get violent visions of Lydia out of her mind.

What had Fisher and Barnes done to her? Was she even still alive?

While Taylor had always wanted to work a case with the big boys, and Lopez was truly a great one to start with, she wished it was anything but this. Lydia needed to be home with her family. But they at least now had another lead, a stolen vehicle that would hopefully bring them closer to the trail. It wasn't much, but eventually the puzzle pieces had to start coming together. The two men couldn't stay hidden too long with their photos being splashed on every news station in the southeast.

As they crossed back into Hart County, Taylor was mentally going through every detail they had so far—the vehicles, the towns, and the dates—doing her best to unravel the latest web of darkness enveloping their town.

CHAPTER 17

The next morning when Taylor walked out to her truck to head to work, she found Sam leaning against the hood, waiting. A manila envelope was in his hand, and he held it out to her, his expression inscrutable. Diesel was running around, sniffing, and peeing on every blade of grass he could get to as though his life depended on it.

"Where's Alice?" she asked.

"With the science homeschool group. Field trip to the museum. I promised her I'd chaperone in the spring when they go to the Atlanta Braves game. I'm not big on science."

If she's with him in the spring, Taylor thought but didn't say out loud.

No matter how long she was with Sam, Taylor was proud of him that he'd sought out help to be sure Alice didn't suffer from being pulled out of public school. He'd found several homeschooling groups and the moms had welcomed them in with open arms. While Alice did most of her work on her own, it was good for her to get around other kids for educational outings to keep up her social skills.

Sam had figured all that out and acted on it himself, most of it while Taylor was busy with work.

"What's going on?" she asked, suddenly worried.

"Read the letter. I don't know what to make of it."

She opened it and pulled out a sheet of paper. On it was a table with two columns, a lot of numbers with some circled in red in each lane.

Sam's name was at the top.

At the bottom it read, "<u>is not excluded</u> as the biological father." The alleged father is not excluded as the biological father of the test of a child. Based on the testing results obtained from analysis of the DNA loci listed, the probability of paternity is 99.9998%. This probability of paternity is calculated by comparing to an untested, unrelated, random individual of the Caucasian population (assumes prior probability equals 0.50)."

She read it again, then one more time, before looking up. By now he was pacing back and forth in front of her truck.

"I think you know what it means, Sam," she said softly. "99.9998% is pretty solid."

He stopped and locked eyes with her. He looked terrified.

"I don't think I'm ready to be a father." Once the words were out, he looked ashamed.

Taylor tucked the paper back into the envelope and laid it on the hood of the truck. She went to Sam and put her arms around him. She could feel him trembling.

"We already knew it in our hearts. Now it's just confirmed," she whispered, trying to calm him. "It will be okay. I promise."

He pulled away and she saw a sheen of tears in his eyes. She loved that he was so sensitive, but it also scared her. The world was hard on sensitive people like Sam.

"Have you told Alice?" she asked.

"No. I haven't told anyone. I read it and couldn't even think. I started worrying about how I'm going to provide for her. Get her a car. Pay for college. A wedding."

Taylor laughed. "Whoa, there. Slow down. She's twelve and you have a long time before all that comes around. What about the custody hearing. Now that you have proof of paternity, I doubt they'll let Derek take her back. I'm sure you'll win custody if that's what you want."

"If that's what *we* want, Taylor," he said carefully. "Remember, we're a team. It's our future together. Either a future with Alice full time, or a future with her part time."

She didn't know what to say to that. It still felt to her like custody was Sam's decision. Not hers. She wanted him to decide alone, so that if it didn't work out it was all on him.

"Anyway," Sam said, still looking nervous. "I need to call the lawyer. No—I won't call. I'll go by his office when I leave here."

She took his hand and held it to her chest. "First, I want you to calm down. Cecil once told me that the world was so obsessed with bad news that we find it hard to realize when something good is happening. I think he's right. We tend to live in survival mode and focus on the bad news that's always crashing over us in waves, while the good gets lost beneath. I want you to really think about this paternity confirmation, Sam. It could be the best news you've ever received. Don't let that joy get buried by fear of the unknown. You will make a great dad. I mean—you are already being a great dad."

He smiled softly, shaking his head.

"How did you end up so smart and why are you with a dummy like me?"

She laughed. "Believe me, I'm not that smart. That's all Cecil. I'm just his little grasshopper. I take in everything he says because without his wisdom through the years there's no telling where I'd be. And you aren't a dummy. Don't ever say that again. Not only are you super smart, but you're a good man. And, in this world, that title holds up more than any college degree money can buy."

"You're too sweet," he said, then kissed her forehead. "I'm

sorry, Taylor. I know you need to get to work, and I've held you up."

"It's fine. I loved walking out to see you standing here, even if you did scare the life out of me with that look on your face."

"I miss you," Sam said, suddenly serious again.

Taylor felt the rush of guilt go through her. He deserved more than she was giving him.

"I'm sorry. I miss you, too, but we're still trying to find Lydia." She didn't know what else to say. Lydia had been gone for nine days now. Days—and nights—that had to be excruciating for her. They couldn't give up.

"Your mom said we aren't having Thanksgiving until you're able to come, when this case is over."

"I heard that. I'm going to try to talk her into not putting it off any longer. It's already a day past Thanksgiving, and I know it's been put on hold for me. But I don't know when we'll find Lydia and I won't be rushing back and forth."

He shrugged. "She's not going to bend on this."

Once upon a time, there was no doubt in Taylor's mind that her job would always take priority, but it was hard to say or even think that now when she had someone in her life who wanted more of her.

Diesel took off at a run and Taylor looked over to see Cate and Sutton walking toward them, Brandy prancing along between them. The two dogs did a circle of sniffing around each other before meeting noses.

Before the women could get close enough to hear, Taylor leaned in, changing the subject back to Alice. Now wasn't the time to debate Thanksgiving lunch.

"We need to make a big deal out of this news for Alice. Maybe have a cake, some presents. Just the three of us. Let me think on it," she said. "And she deserves to know before anyone else so don't say anything to my mom."

He nodded in agreement.

"Mom. Sutton. What're you two doing out so early?" Taylor called out.

"We just checked on the litter of kittens. They're getting big," Cate said, approaching them. "Also looking for Corbin. He should be here soon with Hank for some, as he said, 'Gray family farm time.' I'm going to have him look at Apollo's hooves while he's here."

Sam gave her a quick hug and greeted Sutton.

"Sam, this is Sutton. She's Sheriff Dawkins' niece and she's helping with Mom for a few months," Taylor said.

He already knew who Sutton was but hadn't officially met her. Taylor didn't want the woman to think she'd been talking about her business.

"Nice to meet you," he said politely.

"Likewise," Sutton replied. "I've heard a lot about you."

"Don't believe 'em. I'm a good guy."

They all laughed, and Taylor was glad to see that he was coming down from his panic mode. Sam always had the ability to make everyone around him feel welcome, and, even in his distress, he remembered his manners.

"I've got to go," Taylor said. "I'm a bit late and the sheriff will be breathing down my neck."

CATE and Sutton stood by the fence, petting Apollo. The gentle horse with the soulful eyes had turned himself into one of Cate's farm favorites. Levi had been spending even more time with him since the night of Eldon's rampage—sometimes hours after supper until Jo could get him to come inside—and Apollo had turned into quite the therapy animal.

"He's so gentle," Sutton said, running her hand down Apollo's flank.

"It's gratitude," Cate said. "I've found it's common in animals rescued from horrible situations. They appreciate you more and show more affection. This guy was nearly starving before someone found him behind an abandoned old trailer. The owners moved out and left him. Didn't even notify anyone. How he made it so long must be pure willpower. Now we make sure all his days are nothing but love and care. He's found his dignity again and he'll always be grateful."

"People suck," Sutton whispered as she scratched the horse behind the ears.

"Amen to that," Cate agreed.

She suddenly thought of the dozen red roses and bottle of wine that she'd found on her porch that morning. No card, and she didn't know if they were from Ellis, or if Jackson had ponied up the money to try to win her back. She wouldn't ask, either. Neither of them understood the word no and that she wasn't interested in pursuing another relationship with either of them.

Her heart was now officially guarded.

As she continued to pet Apollo and tell him how magnificent he was, they heard the unmistakable sound of boots crunching on the gravel path behind them. They turned to see a tall man approaching, a large dog trotting by his side. Brandy ran up to the dog and they touched noses and wagged their tails, then ran off together toward the lake path.

"Wow. Who's that tall drink of water with that scary looking dog?" Sutton asked, under her breath.

Cate called out a warm greeting, "Hey, Corbin!"

His hands were full of his equipment, but he nodded back.

"He's a family friend," Cate said. "His dog is Hank, one of our rescues that he adopted. He won't bite."

Sutton squinted against the sun, watching Corbin approach.

"Wait a minute. Did you say Corbin? Not Corbin Eastwood, the country music singer, right?"

Cate chuckled. She observed Corbin through Sutton's eyes and couldn't help but notice that, yes, he was indeed very good-looking in a rough, cowboy way. His faded jeans fit in all the right places, and his weathered boots looked lived in, not just barely scuffed like a wannabe-country-boy wore them. Corbin's face was tan and lined by the sun, in a way that made it obvious he was an outdoors kind of man. The whole package gave off rugged cowboy vibes and she could see why he'd built such a devoted fan base over the years.

"Yes, that's him," she said. "Although he doesn't perform anymore."

Sutton whistled under her breath. "Holy crap. But yeah, now that I think about it, I haven't heard anything new from him in a few years. Wow. My girls would lose their mind if they knew that I was about to meet Corbin Eastwood."

Corbin tipped his hat, and smiled as he drew closer. "Hey there, Cate. How's it going?" He nodded politely at Sutton.

"Hi, Corbin, glad you made it. This is my friend, Sutton. She's staying with us for a while, helping out around the farm."

Sutton extended her hand, her eyes roaming as she took in Corbin's rugged features. "Nice to meet you."

He shook her hand. "Likewise. Always good to meet a new face around here."

Cate opened the gate to the pen and held it, then went in behind Corbin. "Thanks for coming out to deal with Apollo's hooves again. I have a guy who will do it, but Apollo behaves better for you."

Corbin nodded, his attention shifting to the horse. He gave him an affectionate slap on the rear. "Of course. Glad to take a look."

As he examined Apollo's hooves, Cate couldn't help but notice Sutton's subtle admiration of Corbin's strong, capable hands. She stared at him from where she leaned against the fence.

"You know, Corbin, 'Saddle Up My Heart' is my all-time favorite country song. It's got such a soulful tune," she said.

Corbin smiled appreciatively but seemed a bit reserved.

"Thanks. It did what it was intended to do. Brought in a lot of funds. Most don't know this, but 'Saddle Up My Heart' was actually written for a charity event benefiting children with disabilities and equine therapy. It was an honor to be part of something so meaningful."

Sutton raised an eyebrow, intrigued. "That's really nice of you to use your platform for others. Do you have a farm of your own, too?"

Corbin nodded as he continued his work, his muscles creating ripples through the fabric of his shirt as he lifted Apollo's back leg. "Yep, I do. Got a few horses, and I used to ride a few bulls back in the day. But I'm getting too old to bounce back from those falls like I used to."

Cate was amused. This was the most she'd seen Sutton talk yet. She was obviously starstruck. Sutton was older than Corbin, by a decade at least, but it didn't stop her from looking like she'd never seen a tastier-looking man. She leaned in as he talked. "Tell me more about your farm. It sounds like quite the place."

"It's a ranch," he said. "More than a farm because it earns me money." As he described his farm and his experiences with horses and rodeo, Sutton listened attentively, and Cate couldn't help but notice a spark of connection between the two. Despite his rugged exterior, Corbin had a way of drawing people in, and Sutton seemed genuinely intrigued by his stories.

"I love to watch rodeos on television, but I've never been to a real one. Tell us about your most memorable bull-riding experience," Sutton said.

Corbin paused for a moment, still holding Apollo's hoof in his hand as a faraway, wistful look came to his eyes. "Well, there was this one championship rodeo down in Texas. It was a big deal—the kind of event that could make or break a cowboy's career. Every one of my buddies went and half of them entered."

Sutton's eyes widened with interest. "Go on."

He suddenly looked hesitant.

"Yeah, tell us about it," Cate said, though her encouragement wasn't needed. As a matter of fact, she was starting to think she was invisible.

"Okay, what the hell," Corbin began his tale, his voice filled with excitement as he transported them back to that thrilling day. "I was riding this massive bull they called 'Outlaw.' He was notorious for being one of the meanest sons of guns in the rodeo circuit. But I had a feeling that day, you know? Like I was in sync with him from the moment I climbed on his back."

Sutton was hanging on to every word, her eyes locked onto Corbin's face. He'd stopped working on Apollo, giving them his full attention.

"I held on tight, and, for a good while, it seemed like I might actually win that championship." He threw one arm in the air and mimicked holding on to the strap with the other as he pretended to buck wildly. "The crowd was going wild, and I could hear the announcer shouting my name."

Sutton's excitement mirrored Corbin's as she urged him to continue. "And *then?*"

Corbin's expression shifted to a mix of nostalgia and pain. "Well, Outlaw had other plans. Just when I thought victory was within reach, he pulled off a move I'd never seen before and had no idea to anticipate. He bucked harder and higher than any bull I'd ever ridden. In the last few seconds, I lost my grip, and I went flying, along with my chance for that prize money and buckle."

Sutton winced, seeming to feel the intensity of the moment. "What happened?"

Corbin grinned ruefully. "I hit the ground pretty hard, and I heard a few bones snap. But I was still conscious, and I remember thinking, 'Well, that didn't go as planned.'"

Sutton chuckled softly, appreciating Corbin's sense of humor even in a tough situation. "And you didn't win the championship?"

He shook his head. "Nope. That one slipped through my

fingers. But it was the closest I ever came to taking the title. Everyone thought I'd quit after that."

"You didn't want to?" Sutton asked.

"Not at all. That fall may have broken some bones, but it didn't break my spirit."

Cate wondered why he didn't feel the same about his singing. The last time he'd committed to a concert, he'd canceled at the last minute, unable to get over his stage fright. Obviously, he'd rather face a raging bull than an audience these days.

Sutton smiled. "Sounds like you're quite the cowboy, Corbin."

He tipped his hat with a modest smile. "Just trying to live life to the fullest, ma'am."

Corbin talked more about rodeos, injuries, and horses while he finished up with Apollo, and then he stood tall and patted his hands off on his jeans.

"What else you need while I'm here, Cate?" he asked.

"I think that's about it," Cate replied. "You did the goats last time."

"Well," Sutton said, "if he really wants to get dirty, he can help me in the kennels, and cut my chores in half. Then I could take a bit more time making your lunch today, Cate. I have something new I want to try. Corbin, you're welcome to stay, too. I'm making enough for several. It won't be gourmet, but it'll be healthy and delicious, I promise that."

Hmm ... Cate thought. Sutton hadn't mentioned any new recipes when she'd made the grocery list out. She was a sly one.

"Well, that's fine with me. I'm going to go round up Brandy, send Hank back here, then grab a mid-morning nap. Y'all come in when you're done."

They were talking so much, they barely heard her.

Cate laughed to herself. Nothing would probably come of it, as she'd heard from the girls that Corbin still had women from all over the place sending him messages. Most of them trying to forge a love connection. Women of all ages and many of them young and beautiful. Sutton, with her barely any makeup and simple, dark hair cut in an age-appropriate style, was probably way out of his league but, thankfully, Corbin was gentleman enough to be attentive to her.

His mama had raised him right.

Sutton would probably be surprised to hear that Corbin had claimed to be in love with Jo at one time, and even accredited his career to the fact that she'd dumped him, forcing his decision to enlist, where he'd pined after her and began writing love songs in his down time. He'd taught himself guitar and then—boom—had a second career. Of course, now he and Jo laughed about it. He wasn't her type. Not way back then and not now, though Cate wished he was so that he could take Jo's mind off Eldon's betrayal.

Jo's way of coping with troubles was to quietly disappear for a while, according to Taylor. Cate hoped she didn't leave. Having all her girls around her was the one thing that kept her going when everything else failed.

She walked off, heading for the cabin, giving them space to keep up the banter. Corbin had said he needed some Gray family farm time, so that meant he had something heavy on his mind. Maybe Sutton would help him ease it.

On the other hand, Cate couldn't help but feel a sense of satisfaction seeing Sutton open herself to the world beyond whatever it was she was dealing with in the other part of her life, one meaningless conversation and one easy-on-the-eyes cowboy at a time.

CHAPTER 18

As Taylor and Lopez sped toward Athens on the afternoon of November twenty-fifth, the urgency in the car was intense. The call they had received about Barnes and Fisher possibly being spotted at the Georgia Square Mall had their hearts racing. Shane, who had been in his car when the call came through and was half an hour ahead of them, was already on the scene, and Taylor hoped he wouldn't let his impulsive nature get the best of him.

Lopez glanced at Taylor as they weaved through the traffic. "Weaver better not go in like John Wayne and screw anything up."

Taylor smirked. "Let's hope he remembers we're a team."

Arriving at the mall parking lot, they were met with a sea of police cars and uniforms. The scene was chaotic, but Lopez showed his badge, and they were allowed through. They parked and quickly made their way to a sergeant who could fill them in on what had transpired.

The sergeant, a middle-aged man with a stern expression, walked them through the events. "Two hours ago, a suspect we believe is Barnes approached Fran Doblin's fifteen-year-old daughter as she entered the passenger side of their vehicle. He pointed a gun at her, tried to get in the car, and asked for directions to Buford, Georgia. When he saw she was on the phone, he backed off and walked away. The mother called it in."

Taylor's eyes widened as she listened. Barnes was getting brazen approaching people in the broad daylight. Brazen often equaled desperate, a combination that could end in tragedy. The girl and her mother probably didn't realize yet how lucky they were.

The sergeant continued, "Officer Tripp McGarity was nearby when the dispatch came in. He saw Barnes matching the description of the suspect and approached him. Barnes tried to flee, fired a shot into the air, and then turned and fired. McGarity returned fire."

"Anyone hit?" Lopez asked.

"Negative."

Taylor interjected, "Where are they now?"

The sergeant pointed in the direction of the highway. "My guys tracked him to a storage center on Huntington Court, a few miles from here. Barnes jumped the fence and has taken a hostage in one of the units. We've got officers surrounding the area, but I've stayed on scene in case Fisher is still around here. No evidence so far that he is, and I'm headed over there now. Meet you there."

Taylor and Lopez headed back to their car and sped toward the storage center. The presence of police vehicles and officials at the scene was vast, and they could see a line of law enforcement officers taking cover behind their cars, their guns drawn, facing a black wrought iron fence that bordered the rows of units.

They spotted Shane amidst the officials and approached him. Taylor was relieved to see him in one piece, but she could tell he was brimming with excitement. It was going to be hard for him to take a back seat, but this case had become bigger than his small-town detective jurisdiction.

He didn't seem to know that, based on the confidence he exuded while he filled them in. "Barnes has taken a hostage, a man who was unloading his U-Haul truck into one of the units. They're holed up inside, and we can't see them."

Lopez took charge, issuing orders to the officials around them. "Set up a perimeter around the entire property, blocking off that road, too. Make sure no one gets too close. We need to keep the hostage safe."

Everything was a flurry of activity while people got in place, making calls to superiors, setting up barricades, and pushing back the local media who came flocking in sniffing for breaking news.

Barnes had turned the area into a circus.

"How long are we going to let this play out?" Shane asked.

"As long as it takes," Lopez replied. "In a hostage situation, time is the most important factor. It allows the terrorist to calm down, let emotions settle, and even become tired. Then he might begin to be open to negotiation."

Shane said something inaudible under his breath. Of course, he'd want to go in there, guns blazing. Taylor was impatient, too. She wanted Barnes to tell them where Lydia was, but if they killed the man, they might never know.

As night fell, the tension in the air thickened. The sheriff joined them, taking an authoritative role beside Lopez, Athens Chief of Police, Jimmy Sanders, and their Deputy Chief, Brindley. The roar of a helicopter overhead added to the surreal atmosphere, and the distant wailing of sirens filled the background. Snipers took position on the rooftops of the surrounding units, waiting for a clear shot.

Barnes wasn't going to give it to them. He huddled behind stacks of boxes with the hostage always in front of him, the boxes too high to see behind.

Taylor's phone was going off in her pocket, dinging like mad. She only took a glance or two and saw that she had dozens of text messages from Sam, Cate, and her sisters. Quickly, she typed off a reply.

> I'm okay. At standoff with Weaver. I'll check in later. Please tell others.

Grimes had also texted, and called, but she had nothing concrete to tell him yet, so she quickly replied and told him, so far, no eyes or leads on Lydia, but promised an update as soon as possible.

Obviously, there was news coverage going live from above, as well as the vans parked behind the police perimeters who stood by for something exciting to happen. Taylor could just imagine Sam and the others gathered around Anna's living room, watching for a glimpse of her, or for a conclusion to the standoff.

From other communication updates, they kept track of the search for Fisher, who was nowhere to be found, despite the many agencies working on it. Thoughts of Lydia swam in Taylor's mind, taunting her that they were so close to finding her, but what if they didn't?

Lopez continued to use a megaphone, trying to communicate with Barnes, asking him open-ended questions, empathizing with him on how things had gotten out of control, but there was no response.

Weaver, who had left briefly, returned with information about the hostage who had rented the unit. He was a middle-aged man named Dennis Simmons, and he'd moved to the area recently. They called his spouse who was listed as a co-renter on the contract, and they gave her the update that her husband thus far was alive and well and told her to stay put, they'd call her as soon as something changed. They instructed her that, if her husband called her, to immediately dial Lopez on three-way calling so they could talk to him. They got the details they needed from her and put them into play.

"Barnes," Lopez called out on the megaphone. "That man

you've got with you is named Dennis Simmons. He has three adult children and five grandchildren. He's new to Athens and has nothing to do with this. He just retired after spending thirty years working on the lines for Boeing and he's got a little cabin on the river. He's just a working man like you and he's ready to enjoy some time with his family. Some fishing and hunting. His wife, Sophia, is worried about him. Can you let him come on out?"

No reply.

"Please let Dennis call his wife, Barnes. We know you're a reasonable man and you don't want to harm anyone," Lopez lied. "That man hasn't done anything to you."

Still nothing.

"If you're thinking of taking the U-Haul truck and trying to get away, it's not going to happen," Lopez called out. "We've barricaded every angle, and they'll get you through the windshield if you try."

With the hours passing and the standoff showing no signs of resolution, nor any communication from Barnes, Lopez finally issued an ultimatum, his voice reverberating through the night air over the megaphone. "Barnes, I'm not keeping these men out here all night. You have five minutes to surrender peacefully, or we're sending in the SWAT team. I can't guarantee your safety if it comes to that."

The tense wait felt like an eternity.

Three minutes later, Lopez put the megaphone back up to his mouth.

"You now have two minutes, Barnes, then they're storming in like the Marines. You sure you're ready for that kind of ass-kicking?"

"I hope I can get in on it," Shane said under his breath.

Taylor shook her head at him. He wouldn't get close, not with the SWAT team going in like a band of brothers.

"Shoot out the tires on the truck," Lopez called into his radio.

Quickly, in four successive shots that sounded like cannons, the tires were flat. If that had been Barnes' last resort, he was now out of options.

With just one minute remaining on the ultimatum, Barnes yelled out. "I'm coming," he shouted. "Don't shoot. I'm throwing down my weapon."

A sniper on the roof radioed affirmative, that Barnes kicked the pistol out, sending it away from the unit door.

Taylor, Lopez, and Weaver watched intently as Barnes emerged, using Dennis Simmons as a human shield, causing the older man to stumble. He looked exhausted and terrified, his eyes wide with fright as he could finally see all the firepower pointed their way.

Lopez immediately began talking Barnes through the surrender process. "Barnes, come on. Let Dennis go. We don't want anyone to get hurt."

Barnes hesitated for a moment, then released Dennis Simmons, who stumbled away from him, clearly shaken. A few officers ran to him and dragged him out of the way.

"Put your hands in the air, Barnes," Lopez yelled.

Barnes did.

"Turn around."

Lopez continued to call out instructions, ordering Barnes to the ground on his stomach, to cross his ankles and put his arms over his head before a team of six officers rushed in and secured him with handcuffs. He was abruptly jerked to his feet and immediately complained they were roughing him up.

"You haven't seen roughing up yet," Lopez hissed into his ear, plenty loud enough for Taylor and Shane to hear.

Taylor approached, unable to contain her anger. She stepped forward, locking eyes with him. "Where is Lydia Grimes?"

Barnes feigned innocence. "She's with Fisher. She's fine."

Taylor's voice trembled with rage as she demanded, "Where did Fisher take her?"

Barnes shrugged nonchalantly. "I don't know."

"You're going to start talking," Lopez said, then turned to Taylor. "Get directions to the closest precinct. We're taking him in."

Taylor should've felt relief that it was over and exhaustion from the long, tense, wait. Instead, she ignored the fatigue and grabbed onto the new sense of urgency. She couldn't wait to see if they could get Barnes to talk.

Maybe Lydia did have a chance, after all.

CHAPTER 19

The Athens Police Department at two in the morning was a stark contrast to the chaos they had just left behind at the storage center. Taylor, Lopez, and Shane were ushered into a dimly-lit interview room where Barnes sat handcuffed to a metal table after finally being processed.

His clothes looked baggy and unwashed, and Barnes looked defeated, just the way they needed him. The next moments would be crucial in where their investigation led next.

Taylor examined his face and arms, looking for any injuries, but it appeared that he'd been booked in without the ass-whipping he should've gotten. She was never for police brutality, but a small part of her wished that Barnes had *tripped and hurt his face* on the way in. Just a little would've been fine.

They sat down and Lopez immediately took the lead. "Alright, Barnes, let's cut to the chase. We know you've been involved in some serious crimes, and we have evidence linking you to all of them."

Barnes leaned back in his chair, his face a mask of indifference. The handcuffs clanged on the top of the metal table. "I don't know what you're talking about."

Taylor exchanged a glance with Shane, both aware that Barnes was playing hard to get.

Shane decided to take a more direct approach. "We have surveillance footage from Walmart, Barnes. We know you were there with Lydia Grimes. So, don't try to play dumb."

Barnes remained silent, refusing to budge.

Lopez mimicked him, leaning back in his chair, bringing his notebook in front of his face to read from.

"Let's see here," he said. "November fourth, you and your buddy, Avery Fisher, escaped from the Charlotte Mecklenburg jail on foot. Next thing you know, the next morning you're both in Belmont, North Carolina, where you knock on a house belonging to a Mr. Hammond. You feed him a line of bullshit, and he drives around on a wild goose chase until you dump him off in Columbia, South Carolina, and take off with his vehicle."

Barnes stared at Lopez, a small tic in his jaw the only indication of emotion.

Lopez continued. "From there you drive to Myrtle Beach and abandon Hammond's vehicle at a hotel parking lot. You both make your way to the home shared by Trixie Simpson, and her friend, Annette Riker."

"Starting to sound familiar?" Shane said.

Barnes didn't react.

"The four of you drive to Florence for a few days of sex and drugs. On a marathon high, you pick a target and, while the ladies are entertaining him, you and Fisher break into his home and steal his firearms."

Taylor searched his eyes, looking for any piece of humanity, but found none.

"Should I continue?" Lopez asked, pausing to take a sip of his Coke.

Barnes shrugged. "Up to you. I really don't care."

"Listen," Lopez said. "You two have left a trail of breadcrumbs everywhere, and not only have your women sung like canaries, but Fisher's brother, Reggie, did, too. We know it all, other than what you did with Lydia."

Taylor joined the interrogation, her voice firm. "We also found the burned-out car of Serenity Bond, a young woman who was just out shopping with her grandmother. She's still missing, and her family is devastated. They want her back."

Barnes finally spoke, his voice low and gravelly as he shook his head somberly. "I had nothing to do with that girl. That was all Fisher. I told him that wasn't right, what he did."

They pressed on, Taylor trying to appeal to his sudden interest in participating. "Is Serenity dead, Barnes?"

He hung his head, guilt appearing to weigh heavily on him, but he didn't answer.

They shifted the focus back to Lydia, Taylor demanding, "Is Lydia Grimes dead?"

Barnes raised his head, his eyes meeting Taylor's. "The last time I saw Lydia, she was alive."

She couldn't tell if he was sincere or lying again.

Lopez leaned in, his voice stern. "You need to start talking, Barnes. You might be able to pawn off the murder of Serenity Bond on your partner, but, if anything happens to Lydia Grimes, you're looking at the death penalty, even if only accessory to murder."

Taylor hoped that Barnes was as stupid as he looked because that wasn't a true statement. If Serenity was dead, more than likely Barnes would be on the hook with Fisher for that one, too.

Desperation crept into Barnes' voice. "Can we make a deal?"

Lopez's response was unwavering. "We don't have time for a deal, Barnes. If Lydia dies, her blood is on your hands."

"We left her at a small camp we set up at Amicalola State Park, a few hours from here."

Taylor's heart soared with hope, making her lightheaded with relief, but they needed more information. "Amicalola is huge. Be more specific. Give us directions."

Lopez slapped a paper and pen onto the table. "Start drawing a map, Barnes."

Barnes hesitated for a moment before reluctantly picking up the pen. He began to sketch out a rough map, detailing the trailhead near the crest of Amicalola Falls, where they had left Lydia. He gave them information about the initial stretch of the trail, the switchbacks, and some landmarks along the way.

As Barnes provided details, Lopez got on the radio, directing officers to head to Amicalola Park based on the information they were receiving.

Taylor leaned her head toward Shane. "I'm going out in the hallway to call Grimes," she whispered.

He nodded, as though giving permission.

But she wasn't asking.

CHAPTER 20

*A*micalola Falls State Park at four in the morning buzzed with an air of urgency as law enforcement agencies from various jurisdictions converged on the area. Lopez had managed to arrive ahead of Taylor and Shane, and he waved them over to the makeshift command post. A card table under a cheap tent awning served as the epicenter of operations, a large map of the park stretched out, with Barnes' hastily drawn map taped in the corner.

"We're right here," Lopez stated, tapping a spot on the map with a sense of urgency. "Barnes claimed they went up through here." His finger traced a thin trail etched on the map. "We've got a K-9 search team from Hall County on the way. The dogs will be our fastest route to finding her."

A man Taylor didn't recognize approached, and he leaned over the table with an air of authority, scrutinizing the map.

Lopez introduced him, "This is Larry Thompson, the Dawson County Emergency Management Director. He'll be in charge of who goes in and comes out so that this doesn't turn into a search for more than one person."

Thompson nodded and spoke with a tone of caution. "Exactly.

I understand the urgency of the situation, but we must exercise caution. It's crucial to be adequately prepared before sending anyone into the wilderness, especially those without hiking experience. These trails can be treacherous, and we really should be waiting until first light."

"No, we can't wait," Taylor said.

Lopez looked up at her, his eyes narrowed. "There's no *we*. You and Weaver aren't going in. First round will be professional searchers only."

Taylor began to argue but was abruptly silenced by Lopez's raised hand. "Final decision," he declared, putting an end to any further discussion.

"But she's right," Lopez said, directing his comment to Thompson. "From what Barnes has said, she's already been out there a few days. Every minute counts."

"Understood," Thompson said. "Just want you to know the risk you're taking."

Shane remained notably silent, his expression unreadable. Taylor already knew he didn't have much enthusiasm for heading into the woods anytime, especially at night, so she wasn't surprised that he didn't bother protesting.

Lopez then turned his attention to the larger picture. "More teams will be arriving in the morning to join the search effort. We'll have multiple state agencies, as well as local authorities, on hand."

"Do we have any updates on the search for Fisher?" Shane asked.

Lopez provided a quick update. "Two hunters out at South Point Hunting Reserve in Royston reported seeing a black Suburban come down the dirt road near them, then turn around and go the other way. They didn't call it in until an hour later when they heard a report on the radio, but we've got officers in that area searching and setting up a perimeter."

Just then, a K-9 search team arrived, led by a handler of two eager and alert German Shepherds outfitted in orange vests.

The handler introduced himself as Dean Warzack, his dogs straining at the leash.

"These are Bolt and Nova," the handler said, offering a friendly smile. "They're trained in search and rescue. We'll need as much information as possible about the search area."

Lopez pointed to the map and began explaining. "According to Barnes, she was last seen just off the Len Foote Hike Inn trail. That trail eventually leads to a small public lodging that's accessible only by hike, but he claimed they didn't go that far. The trail itself is just under five miles each way, dipping through valleys, rolling across ridges, and passing through green, fern-filled creek valleys."

The dog handler nodded, displaying familiarity with the challenging terrain. "Understood. We'll start from here and follow the trail. If they've strayed off, Bolt and Nova should pick up her scent and I'll call in my coordinates."

With Lopez's approval, Warzack released Bolt and Nova, and the two dogs eagerly bounded off into the woods, their noses to the ground, eager to pick up the scent trail. He followed, walking at a brisk pace.

Taylor wished she had her thick jacket. The temperature had dropped from an unseasonably warm afternoon sixty to a chilly forty-five degrees. She prayed that Lydia was covered. She'd last been seen wearing a coat in the Walmart parking lot, but if she'd been able to keep it was another question.

As they anxiously awaited updates, Sheriff Dawkins arrived on the scene, a mix of exhaustion and frustration etched on his face. He approached the group, his voice gruff, demanding an update.

Lopez promptly filled him in, his tone as confident as possible, given the circumstances. "We've initiated a search operation along the Len Foote Hike Inn trail based on Barnes' information.

We're also keeping a close watch on the South Point Hunting Reserve for any sign of Fisher."

Sheriff Dawkins grunted his acknowledgment, fully aware of the gravity of the situation. "We can't afford to waste any time. Keep me posted." With that, he turned and walked away, leaving the team to anxiously await news from the search teams now deep within the dense wilderness of Amicalola Falls State Park.

Shane turned away to take a call, and Lopez slipped out of his FBI-stamped jacket and handed it to Taylor. "Put this on."

"No, I'm okay," she said, immediately uncrossing her arms from across her chest, pretending she wasn't cold.

"I insist," he said.

Shane turned back just in time to see Taylor slip into Lopez's warm coat. He shot her a disgusted look, then walked away.

Taylor felt like asking him what his problem was, but she wasn't going to stoop down to his childish behavior. This wasn't a time to be juvenile.

Suddenly she felt a tap on her shoulder and turned.

"I'm sorry, I know it was the sheriff's orders, but I couldn't stay away." Grimes was staring back at her, his eyes wide with fear. "Have they found her yet?"

CHAPTER 21

Cate stood at the sink, washing dishes while she listened to the chit chat behind her. Corbin was with them for the second supper in as many days, and Sutton, as promised, had upped her game when it came to making the healthy meals more delicious than they were before he'd come along. Anna would be proud. Or possibly even jealous.

She remembered that Anna was perturbed. Supposedly at just Taylor but Cate could feel some of it directed her way for postponing their Thanksgiving. It couldn't be helped though. She wanted all her daughters around the table. It wouldn't seem like a family holiday without Taylor.

"Come on, tell me about some of your patients," Corbin cajoled Sutton behind her.

"Fine. If you want to be bored out of your mind but I'll pour us some coffee first. Cate, please sit down with us. I'll get those dishes later."

"Nope. Does me good not to be sitting all the time," Cate said. "I'm about to go out of my mind needing more exercise." She didn't tell them the real reason she had so much nervous energy, that she was worried half to death about Taylor, who still hadn't come home since the standoff. Last they'd heard, she was remaining at the state park while teams searched for Lydia Grimes.

They'd been at it all night, and, so far as Cate knew, they'd found no evidence that the woman was anywhere in the park.

"We could always take you for extra physical therapy," Sutton said, winking at her.

"Very funny. I'd rather get back to my work with the animals. Not sit around pumping iron."

Sutton pulled two clean mugs from the dish drainer and poured up the coffee, then took them to the table and sat back down. Judging by the last two dinners, she would rather talk to Corbin about all the places he'd traveled to and how he learned to write songs, but Corbin would only say a bit and then lob the conversation back to Sutton.

It was like they wanted to know everything about each other but tell nothing of themselves.

"Okay, what do you want to know?" Sutton asked him.

"Just pretend I'm thinking of going into nursing. What would you tell me?"

"Hmm ... prepare for long hours and low pay, for starters," she said with a lyrical laugh. "At least compared to the hours you put in to earn it. And you'd better enjoy sitting at a computer because, during and after your rounds, you'll have mountains of documentation to do. Most of it on your own time."

The upside to Corbin being on the farm more than usual was that Cecil had put him to work helping to build another enclosure. The plan was to send the goats and horses back and forth, allowing grass to grow in whichever one the animals left vacant. November had been rainy thus far and they were dealing with a lot of mud, and that meant dirty animals, which made their jobs harder.

Cate could very easily do her chores now, but Sutton

wouldn't hear of it until she had an official, full medical clearance.

Sutton continued behind her.

"Sometimes you'll meet patients who have millions in the bank, but they're so cheap they use the same paper towel all day and steal condiments from the restaurants in town. They'll watch you like a hawk and treat you like a servant. I can't tell you how many times I've cried on my drive home over the years."

"Then why do you do it?" he asked, his question thick with curiosity.

Cate turned off the water and pretended to dry a plate.

She wanted to hear the answer, too.

There was a long pause before Sutton spoke again.

"Because sometimes," she said softly, "you'll meet the nicest people you've ever known, and they'll be sick, but they will want to care for you. Some of the poorest patients will try to minimize their dire situations and offer you their last dollar for being kind to them. And while, yes, you may cry on your way home sometimes, other times you'll laugh all the way about something funny your patient said, or some hilarious predicament you muddled through together. While I see a lot of people at their worst, I also see many at their best. Some days you hate it, and then others you love it because you feel like maybe—just maybe—you made a small difference for one crappy day in someone's life."

"You sound like you do a wonderful job," Corbin said quietly. "It takes a special person to do what you do."

Cate put the plate down and turned around, drying her hands on the towel. She saw that Sutton was using her foot to rub Hank's belly under the table. He was doing the most to help her over her fear of big dogs, being the big teddy bear he'd turned into since he'd first arrived at the farm. Living with Corbin and helping him through his anxiety had given Hank back a purpose in life, and it made him into a happier dog.

"I agree, Sutton. I believe that nurses are born with a unique passion to take care of others, even to their own detriment. It's not something you can teach. It's a gift from God. I also believe that doctors and hospital administrators should have to go on home visits and see what the nurses put up with. Perhaps then they'd be paid what they deserve."

Sutton looked from Cate to Corbin, then burst into tears.

She quickly rose from the table and ran through the room to the door, and then outside.

"What did we say?" Corbin said, his eyes wide with shock.

"Nothing. I think it's whatever is on her mind that she's not saying. She's going through a lot right now regarding her career."

"What? Tell me," he said. "Maybe I can help."

Cate shook her head. "I really don't know the details, but, even if I did, it's Sutton's story to tell. She'll let it out when she's ready and I think she's getting closer. Just keep being her friend. That's all I'm trying to do, too. I feel like she might not have too many in her life right now."

"Cate, I really like her. She's a breath of fresh air compared to most of the women who are interested in me. I deal with so many phonies and Sutton is real. Does that make sense?"

"Wait. You mean you *like her*, like her?" Cate asked, raising her eyebrows.

He laughed. "I don't know. Maybe. Is that weird?"

"Not to me. But some people might think so, just because of the age difference."

"That's not fair. Why is it okay for men to date much younger women, but turn the tables and people talk?"

She shrugged. "It's just the way, I guess. You're only about ten years older than her daughters. Doesn't matter to me, but some may not like it. I'm just saying, if you like her in that way, you'd better be ready for some flack."

He ran his hands through his hair in an irritated motion.

"Well, right now we're just friends. And with any friend I

KAY BRATT

have, I try to help them out of the situations they need someone for. But I can't help if I don't know," he said.

"I understand. Maybe Sutton will confide in you, but I just want to tell you this: be careful. Don't move too fast with her because she's dealing with something big right now. Something that might change your mind about pursuing anything more than friendship."

"You can't give me any idea?" he asked with an earnest look.

"No. Let her tell you. She hasn't even talked about it with me yet. But you are my friend, and I don't want you to get hurt, so, I'm just saying, be careful."

The door opened and Sutton came in, rubbing her eyes.

"I'm sorry, guys. You must think I'm crazy," she said. "But maybe I am. I sure feel like it sometimes."

Corbin stood so abruptly that his chair nearly toppled over. Cate grabbed it.

"No, we don't think that. We think maybe you need to sit down and tell us what is going on. See if we can help," Corbin said.

He went to Sutton and stood in front of her. Then, as Cate watched, he gently brushed a lock of hair out of her eyes, then put his hands on her shoulders.

They stood like that for a moment, as if the only two people in the room, then Sutton backed up and Corbin dropped his hands.

"I'm sorry," he said.

"No—that's fine. I just—I—" she stammered, then sat down on the couch, and put her head in her hands.

Corbin sat beside her, but he didn't try to touch her again. He looked up at Cate, a helpless look in his eyes.

Cate sighed. She wasn't a good talker, and she believed in keeping her business to herself and that everyone should consider doing the same. But Corbin's expression was a plea, begging her without words to intervene.

She went and sat on the other side of Sutton, putting her hand on her back.

"Look, Sutton. We don't want to push you. But if there's something you want to get off your chest, there'll be no judgement here. You never know, maybe one of us can help somehow." She meant that, too. One thing she'd decided, over the short time she'd known Sutton, was that she wasn't a criminal.

And Cate knew one when she saw one.

Sutton finally looked up. "Give me five minutes."

She rose and went down the short hall to the bathroom and closed the door.

Cate heard the water run, then Sutton blowing her nose. Corbin looked frozen in place, as though he was terrified that whatever was said next, it might affect him.

"It'll be fine, Corbin," Cate whispered. "Remember, you're just a friend."

He nodded solemnly.

When Sutton came out of the bathroom and joined them, she was no longer crying. She looked intense, like she was going to war.

She sat down in the recliner, facing them.

"Corbin, you should know that I'm probably going to prison, and, moreover, I'm guilty as charged."

CHAPTER 22

Cate had to hand it to Corbin. Sutton's words did not make him react. At least not visibly. As a matter of fact, she was tempted to go over and take his pulse, for he wasn't moving or even blinking as he stared at Sutton.

"If you'll both just listen and hold your judgment, I'll explain," Sutton said.

Corbin very slowly leaned back until he was resting against the back of the couch.

"You have the floor," Cate said, encouraging Sutton.

She took a deep breath.

"I have a patient and her name is Luella Moore. I've been seeing her at her home for more than a year, since she was diagnosed with a UTI that turned nasty. She also had some other issues with her legs swelling. But while I've been going back and forth, I discovered that her grandson and his wretched wife have been working to make Luella think she's delusional, and they finally filed a petition to be appointed as guardian over her. Next month they plan to have her declared incompetent."

"And you don't think she's incompetent?" Cate asked.

"No. And she's not delusional either. They're after her money.

Her entire estate will go to the little weasel once she's dead, but he's too greedy to wait. He wants it all now. And once he has her declared incompetent, he plans to have her placed in one of the cheapest nursing homes he can find while he takes over her finances."

"I'm not really sure how this story conveys to you doing prison time," Corbin said.

Sutton moved her hands around nervously. "Because I began taking money from her accounts. They call it embezzling."

He looked totally surprised. "You took money from your patient's accounts?"

"Yes, I did," Sutton said stubbornly. "And she gave me permission. Our plan was to start moving it over to somewhere safe from her grandson before he gets his hands on it. He was already nitpicking every penny she spent, so we thought if I took a bit at a time, he might not notice, or he'd think it was to pay my wages. The truth is, she wasn't even supposed to be my patient any longer. Insurance had stopped her home care months before, but I didn't think she was ready to be released, so I kept going. She became my friend, and she needed me."

"Where is the money now?" Cate asked.

"It's safe."

"What were the plans for the money, once you got it?" Corbin said.

"Just to have it where she could get to it without asking permission to use her own money," Sutton said. "Whether it was for a better place to live, or to run away somewhere. Whatever she wanted. It's her money and it's not fair what these greedy relatives do to their elders. I see it all the time and I just didn't want it to happen to Luella."

Cate could tell that Sutton felt passionate about what she was saying, but it didn't make sense. Why would she be arrested if Luella had given her permission?

Corbin beat her to the question.

"Then why didn't Luella just tell her grandson—or the police—that she told you to do it?" he asked.

"She may have. I don't know. They shut me out and slapped a restraining order on me. I can't go near Luella. If she stood up for me, and I'm sure she did, they probably just said she was making up stories because of her dementia."

"Did you try to tell the authorities, and give the money back?" Cate asked.

Sutton shook her head vehemently. "No. Because if I do, he'll get it. I promised her that I'd only give it to her. If she lands in some God-awful place, the money that I got might be her only way out."

"How much did you take?" Corbin asked.

"Fifty thousand," Sutton said, so quietly that Cate nearly didn't hear her.

Corbin whistled.

"I know. I'm in a lot of trouble. But I swear, every penny is accounted for and will be there for her, when I can give it back safely."

"If you transferred it from her accounts, then they have a trail. Why haven't they found it?" Corbin said.

"Because once it hit my account, I transferred it out immediately. Well, in small increments, not to raise any flags."

"So, you have it in cash?" Cate asked.

Sutton hesitated. "I'm not going to say I *don't* have it in cash …"

Her statement settled around them for a moment.

Corbin leaned forward, his brows furrowing with thought. "So, what's your plan now?"

Sutton took another deep breath before answering. "I need to find a way to clear my name and ensure that the money I took goes back to Luella, not her scheming grandson."

"Who is your lawyer?" Corbin asked.

"What lawyer? Remember the twins I told you about? I'm

paying for their college on a nurse's salary because their dad cut them off when they turned eighteen. I can't afford representation. They gave me a court-appointed attorney, but, I can already tell you, he's so wet behind the ears that he isn't going to be much help."

"Sutton, you should've told your uncle all this. He may be able to help you," Cate said. "He sure knows a lot of people in high places."

"Her uncle?" Corbin asked.

"Sheriff Dawkins is my uncle," Sutton said. "But I don't want him to jeopardize his position over this. Luella's grandson isn't just anybody. He's a county commissioner here. So he's got friends in high places, too. Which is how he's working his way through the legal system with the bullshit he's telling on Luella."

"Crooked officials," Corbin said. "I still think that maybe I can help you, but we need a solid plan. Do you have any leads or evidence that could help your case?"

Sutton hesitated for a moment, her fingers tapping nervously on her thigh. "I do have some records and documents that might prove Luella's consent and my intentions. But they're hidden, and I've been afraid to hand them over to my attorney, just in case he's crooked, too."

Cate glanced at Corbin, and they exchanged a silent understanding.

"First things first," he said. "If Luella's grandson is as evil as you think he is, he might send someone over to look for that money, and they could hurt you. You need a safe place to stay while you're trying to clear your name."

"You can keep staying here on the farm for now. It's remote, and we've got cameras now. It'll be safer than for you to stay home alone."

Sutton nodded gratefully, her eyes welling up with tears. "Thank you both. For believing me and not immediately turning your backs on me."

Cate felt herself choking up with emotion. "I've been where you are right now, where I was facing jail because no one believed me. We're in this together, Sutton. But we'll need to be careful and smart about how we handle it."

Corbin stood up, his cowboy boots making a soft thud on the floor. "I'll make some calls and see if I can find a lawyer who specializes in cases like this. We'll need good legal help to navigate through this mess."

"I—can't pay for that," Sutton said, looking from him to Cate.

"Let me worry about that," Corbin said.

Sutton's eyes met Corbin's, and she gave him a grateful smile. "I can't thank you enough for helping me, Corbin."

He tipped his hat and gave her his most charming smile. "Well, ma'am, it's not every day a damsel in distress shows up on my doorstep."

"You mean *my* doorstep," Cate said, and they all laughed.

Sutton looked as though a weight had been lifted from her shoulders, her face instantly younger looking now that she thought she had a chance to prove her innocence.

Cate had suspected there were extenuating circumstances to the charges against Sutton, but she hoped that she hadn't unwittingly opened a Pandora's box right on her own living room floor. The only silver lining she could see right now is that suddenly she had something other than the state of her own affairs—and relationships—to concentrate on. She also had a friend in Sutton. Someone she could trust. She would take both developments as unplanned blessings.

CHAPTER 23

Two days and three nights later and there was still not a shred of evidence that Lydia had ever been in the Amicalola Falls State Park. They still had search teams out there, and at least one K-9 on the ground always, but many of the original people had left, needing to go back to their own jobs or other things.

Taylor was rushing home for a shower because, despite her desperation to be there when Lydia was found, she'd also promised Sam that she'd go to the family court hearing that was scheduled two hours from now.

She couldn't let him down.

Her eyes were heavy and threatened to completely close, and she put her window all the way down, letting the cold air rush into her face and help keep her awake.

When she'd left the state park, they were up to sixty-five people searching, including now *three* K-9 teams. They'd fanned out to more of the trails, as well as the more proficient hikers now searching off trail. They were going into ravines and creeks, too, anywhere and everywhere they could look as they widened the search grid.

Grimes had lost his mind for a while the night before, going against orders as he charged into the woods, searching on his own. Taylor had chased him down and convinced him to go home, be with the girls, and he'd broken down right there off a trail, hitting his knees and covering his face as he sobbed.

She would never get that vision out of her mind. She'd led him back down to base camp, and he'd shuffled like a broken old man, seeming to have aged years in just hours.

She wiped at her eyes as she pulled into the farm driveway. She would love to just go into her cabin and straight to bed, but that was going to have to wait.

She parked her truck and wearily got out and went inside.

Just in case Sam had brought him back, she looked for Diesel, longing for his friendly face and wagging tail, forever thrilled every time she walked into the room.

He wasn't there, and, though she missed him, she was glad he was at Sam's where he could have more attention and less time alone.

Lucy and Johnny weren't there, either. A surprise and a blessing. Taylor didn't have the energy to handle a toddler underfoot, nor to explain to his mama what exactly was happening in the case. She only wanted a half hour of quiet, and to stand under the hot water until all the chill was gone from her bones.

In her bedroom, she undressed and put her gun in the safe, in case Johnny came back while she was showering. She turned on the water and once she'd waited until it was hot, she stepped in and put her face up to the cascading water, exhaling finally now that she was home.

She stood there for the longest time, thinking about Grimes. And Lydia. Their girls. She also thought about Barnes, and how ruthless he'd looked. He had to know more about where Lydia was located. They needed to find a way to make him talk more.

The only good news of the day was that Fisher was in custody.

Moving slowly, she squeezed out some shampoo and lathered it into her hair, then let the water stream over it as she watched the swirls of bubbles fall from her body, landing on her lily-white toes. Her feet ached badly from being in her work shoes for so long.

Fisher had been apprehended just before sunrise, after a high-speed chase by a Georgia State Trooper who had accidentally ended up behind him as he made a pitstop at a rest stop off I-85. The trooper had recognized the Suburban, and after confirming it was the right one, gave chase. Fisher had nearly hit another trooper before evading capture from them both, but a tip was called in half an hour later and they had a team waiting in hiding at the farm his uncle owned in Lula, Georgia.

When Fisher had opened the barn doors to bring the car in, he found himself at gunpoint and had surrendered. They had him in the same jail as Barnes right now, though they wouldn't let the two near one another, to keep them from collaborating on any lies.

According to Fisher, he'd left Lydia tied to a tree somewhere off the trail in Amicalola State Park, though he hadn't given as much detail as to what trail that his partner, Barnes, had. At least with both giving the same general area, Taylor felt like they were hopefully looking in the right place and it would just be a matter of time before they could bring Lydia home.

She turned the water off and stepped out of the shower, leaning toward the mirror to look at her face. Her eyes were bloodshot, and she was paler than usual. She really didn't have time for makeup, but she couldn't show up looking like a vampire, so she hurried through the routine, then dressed in a clean uniform, retrieved her gun, and went to the kitchen.

A sandwich would be great but, when she went to the refrigerator, she saw the time on the oven clock. She grabbed the rest of her things and ran out the door.

TAYLOR SAT with Sam and Alice in the crowded courtroom of family court, the anticipation hanging in the air like a heavy fog. She only had two hours before she had to be back to the department to go over next steps for Lydia's search, and she hoped their case was called soon. Because of how long she'd taken with her shower, she hadn't had time to eat, and her stomach felt like it was eating itself, one groan at a time.

The wooden benches were unforgiving, and the atmosphere was tense as they waited for their case to be called. Taylor watched as Alice fidgeted nervously, her eyes darting around the room, uncertainty etched on her young face.

Taylor could tell that Alice was trying to look anywhere but at Derek, who sat a few rows ahead of them. He'd spoken to them in the hall, and gave Alice an awkward embrace, but it was clear there was no bond between them. Whatever it was that he'd done over the years to make Alice feel unloved, she was holding on to it.

Sam had insisted on having the judge tell Alice about the paternity test result himself. He believed that she deserved to hear the life-changing news directly from the person who would ultimately make the decision that would impact her future.

Taylor was torn on that strategy, but it was Sam's decision and she respected it. This was all new territory to them, and they were learning as they went. And hopefully not screwing up.

The first case on the docket involved a woman trying to be reunified with her children after they were taken due to her neglect. She looked frazzled and frightened, her gaze going constantly between the judge and the children's caseworker at the other table.

"Have you finished going through the drug program, Ms. Chaffin?" the judge asked.

"Yeah. I mean, Yes, sir," she said nervously.

He stared down at her with a doubtful expression. "You know, we've got some research that says moms who struggle with substances might not always be as involved with their kids as they'd like to be. They can sometimes have attitudes that aren't so great for parenting, and they might not know all the ins and outs of how to parent or what to expect from their kids' development. Don't you want the best for your children?"

"Yes, I do," she said. "And I believe what's best for them is to be with me. I've done everything the courts have asked."

"Is that true?" the judge asked the caseworker.

"Yes. She's made every visitation appointment and passed all the random drug tests. She's finished her treatment program and has agreed to continue to attend addiction counseling. The only concern we still have is if she's telling the truth about the boyfriend and whether she's cut ties with him. Because of his violent tendencies and his record, Luther Ross is not allowed to be anywhere near those kids. She has lied to us before and there was a serious incident between him and her eldest son."

"Ms. Chaffin? Can you speak to that?" the judge said.

"Yes, sir," she said, her voice shaking. "I take responsibility for that and I'm sorry. Luther had talked me into giving him another chance, and I fell for it. It won't happen again."

"Where is the children's biological father?" he asked.

"Your honor," the Social Services case worker said, "he's incarcerated for a lengthy sentence and has been for some time."

Taylor watched the young woman hang her head at that statement.

The judge shook his head sadly. He hesitated for a moment longer before giving his verdict. "It is my duty to put the best interest of the children first in my courtroom, and to guarantee their safety. I am not ready to agree to total reunification," he finally said. "I would like to give it another month of visits and you reporting in to drug court. I would also like to see photos of the home the children will return to, including inside, outside, and their bedrooms. It doesn't have to be a palace, but I want to make sure they will be safe. That's it."

He banged his gavel.

Chaffin began to cry, and her case worker shushed her, then led her away from the table.

Another Social Services case was called up immediately, but hers started out badly when the caseworker stated that the mother and father had not yet finished their required parenting classes.

The judge shut his folder and told them they weren't ready to have their kids back, and he shut it down in less than two minutes, then called another as the parents shuffled out of the room.

It was so sad to see how many children were in the system, separated from their parents because the grown adults couldn't be bothered with doing what they were supposed to in order to keep their kids safe.

Alice's case was finally called, and they made their way to the tables in front of the judge's bench. Derek went to the other side with his attorney. His stern expression was mirrored by his lawyer, and Taylor couldn't help but feel a pang of sympathy for him. Soon he would know for sure that Alice wasn't his child, though maybe he'd always known.

Judge Crawford was no-nonsense and began asking questions, his gaze alternating between the two parties. "Why is Alice currently with Mr. Stone, and not with her biological father?"

Sam's lawyer cleared his throat, his voice steady as he explained, "Your Honor, Alice reached out to Mr. Stone during an emergency because he used to date her mother. Sam and Deputy Taylor Gray are in a relationship, and they went to help in the situation. When Alice needed a place to go temporarily, they got official permission to take her to Mr. Stone's home temporarily. Several weeks later, her mother tragically committed suicide, and Alice never felt comfortable staying with her supposed father."

Taylor could see the judge nodding, absorbing the details of their complicated situation. She glanced at Alice, whose eyes were fixed on Sam, seeking reassurance.

Derek's head jerked around at the word *supposed*, an angry scowl on his face.

Alice looked back and Taylor offered her a small smile, silently conveying her support.

The judge continued to question them, delving into the intricacies of their family dynamics and Alice's well-being.

Finally, Sam's lawyer asked if he could approach the bench, and the judge granted him permission. He walked up, holding the manila envelope containing the paternity document. Taylor's heart raced as he handed it to the judge, who began to read it carefully.

Silence hung in the courtroom as the judge's eyes scanned the document. When he finished, he and the lawyer spoke quietly, heads nodding.

He finally looked up at Alice, a thoughtful expression on his face, and then addressed her directly. "Alice, it appears that this finding is something you may have wanted for a long time. It confirms that you are the daughter of Sam Stone. My question to you now is, do you want to live with him permanently, or go back to the home of the man who has acted as your father since your birth?"

Alice's eyes widened in disbelief, her gaze shifting between Sam and Taylor. Sam's eyes glistened with tears as he nodded emphatically, unable to speak.

Taylor held her breath, waiting for Alice's response.

"I knew it," she said, finally, then broke into relieved sobs.

Derek and his lawyer began conversing quietly, their heads dipped toward one another.

The judge's gaze remained fixed on Alice, his demeanor

patient and compassionate. "Take your time, Alice," he encouraged gently.

Finally, Alice turned to the judge and, with a voice filled with emotion, she said, "Yes, I want to live with my dad, Sam."

There were others in the courtroom behind them, waiting on their cases, and the room seemed to collectively exhale as a sense of relief washed over them.

Derek wouldn't turn. He sat like a statue, facing forward.

Sam's tears of joy flowed freely now, along with Alice's, and Taylor couldn't help but join them in shedding a few tears of her own. They had come a long way in their journey to this moment, and the weight of uncertainty was finally lifted from their shoulders.

The judge smiled kindly at Alice and then addressed the court, "In light of this new information and Alice's clear preference, I hereby grant permanent custody to Mr. Sam Stone. Congratulations."

The room erupted in quiet applause, and Taylor, Sam, and Alice hugged each other tightly, a newfound sense of belonging and hope filling their hearts. The journey was far from over, but, in that courtroom, they had taken a significant step toward a brighter future as a family.

When Sam dropped Taylor back at the department building to get her truck, she found Ellis parked next to her, his engine still running. What was it with these men hanging out at her vehicle? Had they forgotten how to use their phones?

He got out when she approached.

"What are you doing here?" she asked, instantly cautious. "Is Cate okay?"

He nodded nervously.

"She's fine. I mean, I guess she is. She hasn't answered my calls for the last week."

Taylor sighed heavily. Ellis was a good guy, at least what she'd known of him. She hated to see his feelings so hurt, but he should've stood up for Cate to his children.

"She doesn't want to come between you and your children," she said, careful with her words.

"I'm not sure why she thinks that's even a possibility," he said. "I know I should've never mentioned to her that they'd expressed some concerns, but Cate took it too deeply. They still trust that I can decide who is in my life or not. And they still want me to be happy, no matter who it is with."

"Then why did you sell your boat?" Taylor asked. "Cate thinks you're moving back toward Atlanta."

He hesitated.

"I've been up to something, but I'd rather show it to you instead of telling you. Do you have some time? Maybe take a ride with me? I'll have you back to your truck within the hour."

She shook her head. "I'm exhausted, Ellis. This case—it's a bad one and they're expecting me back now."

He shifted his weight, foot to foot.

"Please? It would mean a lot and I think you can tell me how to approach Cate about what I want to show you. What about if it only takes half an hour?"

She looked at her watch. She did have time, though she wanted nothing more than to be back with Lopez, helping find Lydia.

Why did she have such a hard time saying no?

He looked so earnest. And Cate seemed lost without him, no matter what she said about wanting her independence and not to be tied down. She missed Ellis, but she'd never admit it. She was so used to being hurt that she'd gone into protective mode to keep it from happening again.

But what if she was missing out on the love of her life? And Taylor could help fix it?

"Fine," she agreed. "But you're taking me through Wendy's for a cheeseburger and a Frosty on the way, and we still have to be back within thirty minutes so you'd better hurry."

A huge smile broke out across his face.

"Done deal. I'll even spring for French fries for dipping. Come on. My chariot awaits."

CHAPTER 24

The lawyer's office in Jasper, Georgia, had an air of solemnity, and the polished mahogany desk dominated the room. Sutton, Corbin, and Cate sat in plush leather chairs facing the attorney, Mr. Anderson, who had been recommended by Corbin due to his expertise in cases involving elder abuse.

Mr. Anderson leaned forward, his glasses perched on the tip of his nose, and he fixed his gaze on Sutton. "Now, Ms. Scott, I want you to start from the beginning. Tell me about Luella Moore and the situation you've been facing."

Sutton took a deep breath and began recounting the story. She described Luella's deteriorating health, her diagnosis, and the genuine friendship that had developed between them. "Luella trusted me, Mr. Anderson. She confided in me about her fears regarding her grandson, Connor Moore, who was after her estate. She showed me how much money he's already taken from her, and she wanted me to help protect her assets."

"Why didn't you seek legal assistance?" he asked.

"She was afraid to. Said he'd find out," Sutton replied.

Mr. Anderson nodded, making notes as he listened. "Tell me

about the actions of Luella's grandson and his wife, Shelly, that you believe are attempts to manipulate and deceive her."

Sutton went on to describe how Luella's grandson had orchestrated situations to make her appear forgetful and confused. "He moved things around in her house, hid items, and then accused her of misplacing them. Shelly even claimed that Luella had started small fires in the kitchen, which were clearly set by Shelly herself. Very coincidental that they only happened when Shelly was there."

Corbin and Cate watched as Mr. Anderson's expression grew more serious with each revelation. He glanced at them briefly, then turned his attention back to Sutton. "Do you have any evidence of these actions?"

Sutton nodded. "I have photographs, documents, and even audio recordings of conversations with Luella where she expressed her concerns about her grandson's intentions."

"Is she aware that she was being recorded?"

"Yes, she agreed."

The attorney's eyes glinted with interest. "That's crucial evidence, Ms. Scott. We'll need to ensure its protected and properly documented."

Sutton handed over a folder containing the evidence she had collected. Mr. Anderson began to examine the materials carefully. "This is a good start. We'll also need to gather witness testimonies to corroborate your claims. Is there anyone else who may have noticed the manipulation and abuse?"

"Not that I'm aware of," Sutton said. "Luella stays to herself. Connor is smart, too. He wouldn't allow anyone else to know what he's doing."

"We'll need character witnesses for you then," he said.

Cate spoke up. "I can vouch for Sutton. She's been staying with us on the farm, and she's been acting as my own nurse. Unofficially."

Mr. Anderson nodded appreciatively. "Having credible

witnesses will strengthen your case, Ms. Scott. Now, regarding the money you took from Luella's accounts ..."

Sutton interrupted, "I swear, I didn't take it for personal gain, Mr. Anderson. I did it to protect Luella's assets from her scheming grandson. I have every intention of returning it to her once this is resolved."

The lawyer regarded her with a thoughtful expression. "We will need to establish a clear trail of the funds and document your intentions. We'll need to involve the police in investigating the financial abuse by her grandson."

Sutton agreed, "I'm willing to cooperate fully and provide all the necessary information to ensure justice is served."

"Have you ever been arrested in the past, Ms. Scott?"

"Never," she said. "Not even a traffic ticket. I've always had a good job and I pay my taxes. I'm not a criminal."

Mr. Anderson leaned back in his chair, looking satisfied with their conversation. "We have a strong case to build upon, Ms. Scott, but it won't be easy. Elder abuse cases can be complex, and, technically, unless we can prove otherwise, you stole her money. However, with the evidence you've gathered, we stand a good chance."

Cate breathed a sigh of relief. It was a long road ahead, but, with a skilled attorney on their side, she felt a glimmer of hope that justice would prevail for Sutton and Luella.

Mr. Anderson tapped his pen thoughtfully against his notepad. "Now, Ms. Scott, you mentioned that they plan to have Luella declared incompetent next month. How do they plan to go about doing that?"

Sutton hesitated, her brows furrowing as she explained, "They intend to obtain a medical opinion stating that Luella is incompetent. I've overheard them talking about taking her to a doctor of their choice."

Corbin and Cate exchanged concerned glances as Mr. Anderson absorbed the information. "That's a serious issue," he said. "We need to ensure that doesn't happen, and that Luella's mental state is accurately assessed by an unbiased medical professional."

Sutton nodded firmly. "I agree. I've been looking into it, and I believe we can preempt their efforts."

The attorney leaned forward; his interest piqued. "Please, go on."

Sutton explained, "Luella currently has a trusted medical professional overseeing her care. Dr. Stevens has been treating her for years, monitoring her overall health. I've been in contact with him, and he's willing to provide a detailed medical evaluation of her mental state, stating that she is of sound mind and not incompetent."

Mr. Anderson raised an eyebrow. "That will be crucial, Ms. Scott. We should ensure that Dr. Stevens' evaluation is well documented and that we have it on record before they attempt any assessment of their own that can be manipulated."

Sutton nodded in agreement. "I've already spoken to Dr. Stevens, and he's also willing to testify in court if necessary."

Cate chimed in, "Dr. Stevens is a respected physician in our community, known for his integrity. His testimony will carry weight."

Corbin added, "And with the evidence Sutton has gathered, including the audio recordings, we'll have a strong case to challenge any false claims of incompetence."

Mr. Anderson looked satisfied with their approach. "It seems like we have a plan to counter their efforts effectively. The key will be to act swiftly and decisively. We'll coordinate with Dr. Stevens and ensure that his evaluation is submitted promptly. In the meantime, I'd like to be able to set up an interview with Mrs. Moore. How could we do that without raising suspicions from her grandson?"

"I can't help with that," Sutton said. "They slapped a no contact order on me. I can't visit, call, or even contact her online."

"But I can," Cate said. "They don't know who I am. I can go check on her, see what's going on and report back. If you will, Sutton, tell me where she lives and give me an idea of what would get her to open the door and let me in."

Sutton nodded, determination in her eyes. "I know just the thing and I'm ready to do whatever it takes to protect Luella and clear my name. Her scheming grandson cannot be allowed to succeed."

As they continued discussing their strategy, Cate was filled with a new surge of energy. Something like she got when she was working to protect her friends behind bars from other inmates who tried to exploit them. Her long sleeping Mama Bear mode was coming out and ready to roar.

CHAPTER 25

Back in the dimly lit interview room at the Athens County jail, Taylor, Lopez, and Shane huddled around a large map of Georgia, mounted on a bulletin board.

Taylor felt torn between wanting to be there, discussing tips and strategies, and wanting to be with the teams searching the Amicalola trails. At this point, she was so exhausted that she was surviving on small naps snatched here and there—and pure adrenalin.

Lopez pointed to the town of Madison on the map, his finger hovering over the marked location. "The truck was found there," he explained, his voice laced with frustration. "Parked in an old junkyard next to other vehicles, like they were trying to make it blend in."

Taylor's brow furrowed in thought as she contemplated the peculiar choice of location. "It doesn't make sense. Madison is located right next to the Oconee National Forest. If the intention was to leave Lydia on a remote trail, why didn't they do it there instead of going all the way up to Amicalola?"

"They left the truck before they grabbed her from Walmart," Shane said. "Somehow, they made their way from Madison, down to Hart's Ridge, then over to Athens. No way she's in Oconee National."

Sheriff Dawkins, a weary expression etched across his face, entered the room with a heavy sigh. "Lord, I hope that forest isn't a possibility. It spans nearly 900,000 acres across twenty-six counties. Searching for her there would be like finding a needle in a haystack."

"Barnes is the more talkative one, and he's swearing he's told the truth." Taylor said. They'd also interviewed Fisher earlier that morning, and he'd collaborated Barnes' claim that Amicalola was where they'd left Lydia.

Lopez, his arms crossed over his chest, nodded slowly as he pondered their limited options. After a tense moment of silence, he spoke, determination ringing in his voice. "Well, let's get him out of the cell and take him to Amicalola. He can lead us to her."

THE TRAILHEAD near the crest of Amicalola Falls greeted them with the soothing sound of rushing water, a stark contrast to the grim situation they were in.

Barnes wore a county jail orange jumpsuit, his wrists secured in handcuffs. He glanced around uncertainly, his eyes scanning the dense woods around them. "It's up here somewhere," he muttered, then stumbled over a tree root.

Lopez caught him before he could fall. He and Shane took turns leading him, never letting go of his arm. Taylor followed closely behind, her eyes darting between Barnes and the rugged terrain.

"We're not turning back if you bust up your face, so you'd better be careful," Lopez said, jerking Barnes upright.

"What about Avery?" Barnes said. "Did he give you any directions?"

"Don't worry about Fisher," Lopez said. "This is your mission, and, if we bring Lydia Grimes out of here today, it'll look good for you in court."

Taylor, this time more prepared for the unpredictable Georgia weather, had her thick county jacket on, and followed closely behind, ready to grab Barnes if he tried to get loose and double back toward her.

Shane was behind Lopez and, never one to hide his complaints, grumbled about the challenging conditions, prompting Lopez to offer some tough love.

"Man up, Weaver. We're not here for a leisurely hike."

They continued along the trail, passing the point where it swung right at 0.35 miles, departing from the Appalachian Approach Trail. The path began to ascend, taking them through a series of switchbacks that tested their endurance.

As they hiked, Barnes led them further, veering east through a dense forest filled with young tulip trees and towering oaks. The steady climb brought them to a small knob at 0.8 miles, where they were treated to breathtaking views of the rolling southern Appalachian mountains through the forest's tree line.

Taylor couldn't help but marvel at the natural beauty around her, even as the thought of Lydia being out there somewhere, thirsty and hungry, weighed heavily on her mind.

Pressing on, they encountered stretches of sandy, moss-covered forest floor, their feet sinking into the soft ground. At 1.6 miles, they reached a massive, ancient tulip tree, its imposing trunk standing tall among the surrounding trees. Taylor's internal thoughts wrestled with the contrasting emotions of awe for the majestic tree and the despair of Lydia's predicament.

They took a much-needed break, sipping water from their bottles and questioning Barnes about the surroundings. Barnes appeared lost and unsure, which only fueled Taylor's suspicion that he might be lying or confused. The hike had begun to take its toll on them, with branches slapping their bodies as they trudged through the thickets.

The trail led them to a small summit at 2.1 miles in, revealing a broad ridge ahead through the forest canopy.

Lopez turned to Barnes and asked, "Did you take her to the ridge?"

Barnes turned in a circle, breathing heavily, his gaze flitting between the trees. He pointed to a tall tree about twenty yards away, just off the trail. "No. It was right here," he said, his voice trembling.

They went to the area he'd pointed out and Taylor's heart sank. She'd let herself hope that today would bring Lydia home, but now doubt crept in again. There was no evidence that anyone had been near it, no sign of Lydia's presence, or footprints from anything human.

Frustration boiled over, and Shane cussed as he kicked the tree.

Lopez pushed Barnes up against another tree, his voice laced with anger. "You're leading us on a wild goose chase!"

"No, I'm not," Barnes protested. He turned again, looking back at the trail they'd left, "Maybe I've got the wrong area."

Lopez pulled a small map from his pocket and handed it to Taylor, his voice edged with frustration. "Spread it out on the ground."

Taylor complied, unfurling the map before them.

Lopez jerked Barnes down to his knees to look at it.

"Damn, don't be so rough," Barnes yelped, then stared at the map.

Shane bent down beside them, pointing. "This is where we are now." He moved his finger. "Here's where we came in. Are we on the right trail?'

Barnes nodded. "I think it is, but maybe Fisher came back here before you guys got him. He could've taken her somewhere else."

"You're a damn liar," Shane said. "You know where she's at. You probably killed her yourself."

That was Taylor's biggest fear; that Barnes knew Lydia was dead because he'd helped murder her, then left her body somewhere else in the vast wilderness. She pushed away thoughts of packs of coyotes coming upon her.

Barnes' face contorted with fear and guilt as he vehemently denied any involvement in Lydia's death. "I swear, I didn't kill her. I don't know where she is," he pleaded, his voice cracking.

Taylor exchanged glances with Shane and Lopez, both silently acknowledging the possibility that Barnes might be buying time or playing mind games.

Lopez's expression was stern and unyielding. "Listen to me carefully, Barnes," he said, his voice low and menacing. "If you're lying or holding back any information, if anything has happened to Lydia, you're sealing your own fate. You'll face the full force of the law, and you won't escape the death penalty."

"You ready to feel the poison race through your veins?" Shane asked.

Barnes' eyes darted between the determined faces of Lopez and Shane. He seemed to be grappling with an internal struggle, torn between the consequences of revealing the truth and the consequences of keeping it hidden.

Finally, he broke down. His shoulders slumped, and he hung his head in defeat. "Okay, okay," he mumbled. "Fisher will kill me but I'll tell you everything. First, I need some assurance. Protection. You can't let me go to the same prison as him."

Lopez clenched his jaw, clearly torn about negotiating with a suspect. "We don't have time for deals, Barnes," he retorted. "You're running out of chances here."

Desperation painted Barnes' face. He took a deep breath and began to divulge what he knew. "We left Lydia at a small camp we set up near a creek. It's not far from here, I promise."

Taylor leaned in; her eyes locked onto Barnes'. "Tell us more. Be specific."

Barnes hesitated for a moment, his gaze darting to the ground as he retraced their steps in his mind. "We didn't go this deep into the woods. It was just off the trail about a mile in. Fisher saw a creek nearby, and he thought it would be secluded enough. I swear, that's where we left her."

Taylor's heart raced with a mixture of relief and anticipation. They finally had a lead, a specific location to focus on. "We need more details, Barnes. Tell us everything you remember about the camp and the surroundings."

Barnes nodded, and his voice quivered as he recounted the details of their makeshift campsite. "Not much of a camp. We set up a small fire pit with rocks and slept on the ground between a couple of trees. Fisher tied her up and we left her with some water and food. She was scared, but she was alive when we left."

"When did you leave her? This time, don't lie," Lopez said.

"I—I guess about two days before you all cornered me," Barnes said. "We'd gone to that mall to find some new wheels and we planned to come back and get her. Fisher said she would be a good bartering tool if and when we needed it."

Lopez signaled to them over Barnes' head, nodding.

He jerked him to his feet.

"Show us."

Barnes took one more look at the map still on the ground, then turned east and started walking, Lopez's hand tightly woven around his bicep. Their reluctant guide damn well better lead them to where Lydia had been left behind this time.

CHAPTER 26

Cate stood at the doorstep of Luella Moore's quaint little home, clutching a small, black kitten with white socks in her arms. The chilly Georgia breeze rustled her hair as she took a deep breath, her heart pounding with anticipation. She had never met Luella before, but she was here on a mission to earn the elderly woman's trust and help Sutton's case.

With a gentle knock on the door, Cate waited anxiously. After a few moments, the door creaked open, revealing a frail, silver-haired woman peering out.

Cate put on her warmest smile and said, "Hello, ma'am. I was doing my evening walk and found this poor kitten in the street, huddled under a parked car. I was wondering if I could bring him in to warm up and maybe give him a little milk."

Luella's eyes softened as she looked at the kitten in Cate's arms. "Oh, the poor thing. It looks just like my old cat, Socks. Come in, dear."

Cate stepped inside the cozy living room, cradling the kitten gently. Luella led her to a small, well-loved armchair, and they settled the cat in Cate's lap. The feline purred contentedly and began kneading its paws, gradually drifting off to sleep.

Luella bustled out of the room, returning with a warmed bowl of milk for the kitten, and then offered Cate a cup of hot tea.

Cate accepted gratefully, and Luella left again.

The kitten lapped at the milk hungrily.

When Luella returned, she was holding an old-fashioned tray with a tea kettle and mugs. She poured, then sat down on the couch.

The warmth of the tea soothed Cate's nerves. She was about to disclose her deception.

She put the cup down and said, "Mrs. Moore, there's something I need to tell you. I don't really live on this street. I'm a friend of Sutton's, and she's very worried about you."

Luella's eyes widened in surprise, then she looked up and down the street, a frightened look on her face. "Sutton? Is she okay? I haven't heard from her in so long, and I'm terribly sorry for what my grandson, Connor, has done to her."

Cate nodded sympathetically. "Sutton is doing her best, but she's in a difficult situation. She's facing legal trouble because of Connor's actions, and she's worried about what he might do to you. She wants you to know that all the money is exactly where you two discussed it would be."

"Oh, I know that. Sutton is no thief." Luella's face crinkled with concern. "I knew that Connor was up to no good, and then he discovered what we'd been doing. I was afraid of what he would do if I tried to go against him. He's my family, and I didn't want to believe he would hurt Sutton like this. I told him that she did not take my money. That I allowed it, and she plans on giving it back. He won't listen to a word I say. Treats me like I'm a child."

Cate reassured her, "We have an attorney ready to represent Sutton, and we also have a statement from your regular doctor stating that you are competent and do not need a conservator. We want to help clear Sutton's name, but we also would like to protect you from any harm."

"Shelly," Luella said, her mouth contorting like she was tasting something bitter. "Connor has turned into someone I don't recognize since he married that girl. She broke up his first marriage, you know. That was a good woman, but then Shelly came swinging those hips around the office where Connor works, and, next thing you know, he's divorcing his wife and taking up with Shelly. He ought to be ashamed. She'll ruin him."

Cate sipped her tea while cradling the purring kitten in her arms, her attention focused on Luella as she ranted. She appeared to be very intelligent, and she didn't stumble over words, nor look lost for thoughts.

Luella let out a heavy sigh, her wrinkled hands trembling as she reached for her teacup. "Anyway, I don't know if anyone can save me. You see, dear, Connor and Shelly, they've been doing all sorts of things to make me seem forgetful and confused. It's been a nightmare and I know I'm headed for a bad place. Shelly's already telling me I'd better have my bags packed. And I don't want to leave my home. Not yet, when I'm fully capable of living here alone."

Cate leaned in attentively, encouraging Luella to share. "Tell me more, Mrs. Moore. We need to know everything."

With a weary look in her eyes, Luella began, "They've been rearranging things in my house when I'm not looking. I'll put something down in one place, and the next day, it's nowhere to be found. Then they accuse me of misplacing it. It's been happening for months, and I knew something was amiss."

Cate's heart ached for the elderly woman. "That's terrible. What else have they done?"

"Connor took me to some doctor he scraped up, then stood right there and told the man that I don't bathe, I don't sleep, and I wander all over the neighborhood. It's just not true!" Luella continued, her voice quivering, "And Shelly, that blasted woman, she claimed I started small fires in the kitchen. They always happened when she was around, like she was setting them herself. She must've because I know I didn't do it."

Cate nodded, absorbing the information. "That's deeply troubling, Mrs. Moore. We'll make sure to document all of this."

"That's not all. I'm embarrassed to even tell you this but late one morning Shelly told me that she was going to take me shopping. We drove my car to the plaza, and she dropped me at the door and told me to go inside, that she would park. She never came in. I finally called her, and she accused me of taking the car from the garage myself, driving to the plaza, parking it, and leaving the keys in it. Said I was forgetting that I did it. I'm not crazy, I know what she did. She took a taxi home and then called Connor with this crazy story. Or he helped her invent it."

Tears welled up in Luella's eyes, and she clasped her hands together. "I didn't want to believe my own blood would do this to me, especially after all I've done for him. I've bailed him out with money his whole adult life, but it's clear they're after my entire estate. I just wish there was something I could do to make up for everything involving Sutton. She's such a nice girl."

Cate reached out and patted Luella's hand gently. "We're going to help you, Mrs. Moore. The attorney will work to set things right. Can you go with us to meet with him? Maybe tell your grandson you're going to the senior center for potluck and bingo?"

Luella's gratitude was palpable as she looked at Cate with renewed hope. "That sounds like a good idea. Thank you, dear. I don't know what I would have done without Sutton for all those months. And now she's in so much trouble. I will cooperate fully and do whatever it takes. You must be careful, though. Those two are crafty little foxes. They'll have me in a home so fast it'll make my head spin."

She rubbed the cat's ears and cooed to him.

Cate nodded confidently. "You leave it to us. We'll make sure you're safe and that your grandson is stopped."

As they continued their conversation, Cate couldn't help but feel even more committed to their cause. She knew that exposing

Connor's deceit and ensuring Luella's well-being were challenges, but the woman's safety was worth it, especially if it helped clear Sutton.

Tears welled up in Luella's eyes, and she grasped Cate's hand. "Oh, bless you, dear. You have no idea how much this means to me. I'll do whatever it takes to set things right."

Cate smiled warmly. "We'll arrange a meeting with the attorney in two days, first thing in the morning. You should step out of your house and walk to the end of the road so that no one sees us pulling into the driveway. We'll pick you up there."

"Oh, isn't this going to be exciting," Luella exclaimed, a devilish grin creeping onto her face. "We're going to outfox the fox."

As Cate watched Luella cradle the peacefully sleeping kitten in her lap, she hated to tell her it was time to take it back. But Luella must have sensed it because she gently lifted the little creature and handed him over.

"The kitten was a nice touch," she said, smiling with a sparkle in her eye. "I'd ask to keep him, but I know that Connor would just take him away from me. Even if he let me keep it, I'd have to beg for the funds to take care of him. Maybe once this is all settled, you could help me find another one."

"I'll do better than that, Mrs. Moore. I'll hold this one for you, and, as soon as you're ready, I'll bring him over along with all the things you'll need to take care of him. You be thinking of a good name, okay?"

Luella clasped her hands together tightly, smiling in anticipation. She looked like a little girl at Christmas who had just been given her favorite gift.

CHAPTER 27

The rain drummed relentlessly against the courthouse vestibule's roof, creating a dissonant symphony of water droplets. Taylor stood beside Special Agent Lopez, her eyes hidden behind a pair of dark sunglasses, despite the dark day. She didn't want anyone to see how emotional she was that the conclusion to the search for Lydia was not what she'd hoped for.

The press conference was a necessary formality, but her thoughts were still consumed by their fruitless search the previous day in the unforgiving wilderness of Amicalola Falls State Park. She replayed their trek through the woods, Barnes leading them deeper into the dense forest with each step, seemingly unsure of where Lydia had been left behind.

Reporters jostled for positions, and the noise of the crowd swirled around her. It felt like the whole crowd had come out, hoping they had good news to deliver.

Thankfully, Grimes and his daughters weren't there. Taylor had gone to their home first to break the news before they told the public. It made her feel sick at her stomach to see them all turn away from her to huddle and cry.

Barnes had led them to a creek, but it felt accidental, and

there was no evidence that anyone had camped there recently. He was either very bad at navigation, or he was a cold-blooded liar.

They'd berated him for wasting their time and resources.

Later, on the way out, Barnes had spoken and told them that, "hypothetically," Fisher had raped Lydia, strangled her with her purse strap, then slit her throat. He said, knowing Fisher like he did, they needed to search all the surrounding cemeteries, and look for a Liz Claiborne purse strap.

Teams searched every graveyard within fifty miles each way and found nothing. They'd never know if he'd made up that story, too, or if they just hadn't found the right cemetery. That detail would not be released to the public yet.

When they'd returned Barnes to the jail, Lopez had thrust him so hard into the cell, that Barnes had fallen on his face, smacking the concrete with a heavy thud before he'd scrambled to his feet and cussed them through the bars.

They'd brought Fisher out again, begging him for information, but he refused to speak.

They were all angry. Tired, too. They'd come out of Amicalola covered in bug bites and scratches from brambles and branches, exhausted, with nothing to show for it. Other teams had stayed behind, searching the area for miles around the creek, until the storm broke out and forced everyone off the trails.

Special Agent Lopez stepped up to the microphone, commanding the attention of the gathered media and curious onlookers. Taylor watched as he began to speak, his tone measured and authoritative. "As we all know, Lydia Grimes of Hart County, Georgia, hasn't been seen in the two weeks since November 15th when she was abducted in the parking lot of a Walmart in Hart's Ridge, Georgia, which later, after a tip, sparked a massive search of the Amicalola area."

Cameras snapped and flashed, recording every word and movement, but Taylor's thoughts remained focused on their struggle to find concrete evidence of Lydia's presence in the park.

"Since November 26th, Dawson County Fire and EMS, along with the Dawson County Sheriff's Office, and more than a dozen State of Georgia resources have actively searched by ground, air, water, and canine over 1000 acres in and around the Amicalola Falls State Park for Lydia Grimes," Lopez continued. "The terrain is very rugged and difficult to navigate but the teams persevered. In two weeks, there has been only one K-9 hit on her scent, and that was in the 3600 block of Highway 52 near Amicalola Falls. The dog lost the trail soon after."

Audible groans of frustration rippled through the crowd, echoing the sentiments of those who had invested their time and resources into the search.

Taylor's turmoil ran deeper. She knew that Barnes had led them on a wild goose chase, creating a web of deception that had them chasing shadows in the forest. The futility of their efforts gnawed at her, telling her they should've spent their time looking somewhere else.

But where?

Lopez gestured for Larry Thompson, the Dawson County Emergency Management Director, to take the microphone. His presence signaled a shift in the conference, and there were more flashes from the cameras. A newswoman from Atlanta tried to elbow her way closer, causing the local reporter from the Hart's Ridge Herald to hiss something at her and hold his ground.

"Because of the rain and the substantial weather damage already today, the staircase leading up to Amicalola Falls has been closed off, and any further searches would have to be rerouted away from the falls and where the dog picked up the scent," Thompson explained.

A reporter seized the opportunity to seek clarity. "What are you trying to say, Mr. Thompson?"

Thompson continued, his voice filled with regret. "At this time, we are suspending the active search unless, and until, any additional information is revealed. There are other places and victims who depend on the same resources we've been using to try to locate Lydia Grimes, and we can't keep them at Amicalola forever."

A collective sense of dismay swept through the crowd, mirroring Taylor's own feelings of helplessness. The realization that the search had come to a halt was a heavy blow for everyone in town, not just those who loved Lydia.

Lopez took the microphone once more, his face fixed with grim determination. "Lydia Grimes is forty years old, five foot nine, and approximately 135 pounds. She has shoulder-length hair, no tattoos or identifying marks. We ask anyone visiting Amicalola State Park to keep an eye out for her on trails or roads. Anyone who sees Mrs. Grimes or someone who resembles her description is urged to call the FBI tip line."

As the press conference concluded and reporters dispersed, Taylor couldn't shake the feeling of despair. The rain continued to pour, a somber backdrop to the conclusion of the search to bring Lydia Grimes home, and Taylor held back the tears that would fall as soon as she was free of the crowd.

CHAPTER 28

Back in Mr. Anderson's office, Cate, Corbin, and Sutton leaned forward, eager to hear what the attorney had uncovered regarding Luella's grandson, Connor Moore.

He had met Luella, and, like them, was enamored with how sweet and sharp she was. He agreed that there was nothing about the woman that pointed toward needing a guardian or conservator, and he'd gotten started right away in his investigation into Connor Moore.

Now they were ready for the update.

Cate tried to keep her concentration on the task at hand, but she kept thinking of Taylor, and how sad she'd been that morning before leaving for work, depressed that they had failed to find Lydia Grimes.

The press conference was happening right now back in town.

It was simply tragic, and Cate couldn't imagine what her family was going through as she'd silently thanked the heavens above that it wasn't one of her daughters who had been snatched.

Mr. Anderson adjusted his glasses and began, "I've been using my connections to dig into Mr. Moore's background, and what

I've found is rather intriguing. It seems that he is more deeply entangled in a web of corruption than we initially thought."

Sutton exchanged a surprised glance with Cate and Corbin. "Corruption? What do you mean?"

The attorney leaned back in his chair, his expression serious. "Connor Moore is connected to a major land development scandal in your county. Not only is he putting together yet another housing project that the people of your county don't want, but he's been working hand in hand with another county commissioner who holds a significant influence over land development decisions. At this time, I'll not disclose the name of his colleague. We might need that later."

Cate raised an eyebrow. "What kind of scandal are we talking about?"

Mr. Anderson leaned forward again, outlining the details. "Both county commissioners at the center of the scandal have been secretly accepting bribes and kickbacks from developers and builders in exchange for favorable zoning changes, expedited permits, or access to valuable land."

Sutton's eyes widened with realization. "So, Connor needs more seed money to pour into these cookie-cutter subdivisions that are popping up around here. That's why he's trying to take control of Luella's estate early."

The attorney nodded. "Exactly. It appears that he is part of a network of developers and business interests benefiting from these land development deals."

Corbin leaned in; his interest piqued. "Do we have any idea who the whistleblower is or how this scandal came to light?"

Mr. Anderson paused, considering. "That's just it. It hasn't come to light yet. I can only tell you that it's someone within the commissioner's office with insider knowledge. This potential whistleblower may have access to incriminating documents, emails, and/or recorded conversations that implicate the two commissioners and others."

Sutton couldn't help but feel a glimmer of hope. "If we can somehow find and secure evidence related to this land development scandal, it could be a powerful bargaining chip in our fight against Connor."

The attorney nodded, clearly thinking along the same lines. "Indeed. It could be used to pressure him into backing off from Luella's affairs. However, we must tread carefully. We don't want to alert him that you all have this knowledge."

Cate was excited that the attorney had dredged up something useful. Now, they just had to decide how to use it. "What's the plan, Mr. Anderson?" She asked.

He leaned back, steepling his fingers. "I propose that I approach Connor with this information discreetly. I'll give him the option to back out of Luella's business entirely, including signing that he'll forfeit any future opportunities to claim guardianship or conservator over her. He will also have to agree to drop the charges against you, Ms. Scott, and give an official statement that his accounting was wrong. If he agrees, we'll refrain from pursuing legal action related to the corruption scandal. If he refuses, we blow the whistle."

Cate didn't like that Connor had an opportunity to continue being corrupt, but stopping that situation wasn't their goal. Keeping Luella safe and Sutton out of jail was the directive that they could handle. Hopefully, later down the line, someone else would make sure Connor got what he had coming.

Sutton frowned, skeptical. "Do you think he'll actually agree to such a deal?"

Mr. Anderson shrugged. "It's hard to predict, but people in his position often prioritize self-preservation. If he believes we have damning evidence against him, he may see it as the lesser of two evils."

Corbin chimed in, "What if he refuses?"

The attorney's gaze turned steely. "If he refuses, we'll have no choice but to proceed with our original plan, using the evidence we've gathered so far to protect Luella and bring her grandson to justice. Unfortunately, in that scenario, we will not be able to help Ms. Scott with her legal troubles."

Sutton took a deep breath, her resolve firm. "Let's do it. Even if I still go to jail, we can't let Connor continue to manipulate and exploit Luella. She doesn't want him in her life. Not now or ever, after everything he and Shelly have tried to pull."

"If she cuts her grandson loose, she'll need to decide who will be there to help her in the future, when she does need guidance," Mr. Anderson said.

"I'll talk to her about that. I know that she has a niece who is a well-respected professor at Georgia Tech. She might want her," Sutton said.

Mr. Anderson nodded. "Very well. I'll arrange a meeting with Connor and present him with our offer. In the meantime, I'll continue to gather more evidence related to the land development scandal. We need to be prepared for any outcome."

"What if you approach him, and he goes straight to Luella and harasses her?" Sutton said.

"I'm going to take care of that," Corbin said. "Mr. Anderson, if you tell me the date and time that you'll be meeting with him, I'll have someone sitting outside Luella's home, watching and ready to intervene in case Moore goes there and reacts badly."

"Corbin," Sutton said. "You can't do that. You've already stepped up to pay for this part of the situation. I can't let you come out of your pocket for more."

"You can, and you will. It's like this," he said. "If I have the ability to protect someone from a bully, I'm going to take it. When I was younger, I did some not so cool things. Especially at school, and I wish I could take it back. These days I take every opportunity I can to try to balance the scales in my favor, to make up for being an asshole."

"That's very kind of you," Mr. Anderson said.

"Oh, it's going to be a long journey, believe me. Or just ask some of my ex-girlfriends." Corbin joked, and they laughed.

Cate loved that she was also getting to be a part of putting Luella's grandson in his place. She'd had more than her share of dealing with corrupt officials when she was in the penal system, and to be in the front seat to see one of them be squashed was enticing.

But they would have to be careful.

This wasn't something to take lightly, she knew that, too. The stakes were high because if Connor found out that Cate was a part of any of it he could make things hard for the farm and their business. He had connections, obviously, but it was worth the risk, and she had a feeling that if she put it on the table for all her daughters to discuss, they'd agree.

It wouldn't go that far, hopefully, because she also knew another thing. If Taylor found out there was exploitation going on in her town—and the county she represented—she'd take a dive right into the middle of it and endanger herself and her career. This one was going to have to stay under the radar, and they'd have to let karma take the trash out eventually.

CHAPTER 29

The relentless rain had stolen the joy from the world outside, and, as Taylor awoke in Sam's comfortable bed, she couldn't help but feel the weight of the gloomy morning pressing down on her. Her thoughts drifted back to the fruitless search for Lydia, the ache of disappointment and hopelessness still gnawing at her. The tragic look on Grimes' face when they had to tell him the search was called off. It was all still on her mind, and her emotions were all over the place.

Serenity Bond was also not found yet, though the search still continued in her area, but it wasn't looking any better for her than it did for Lydia.

Stretching her tired limbs, she sat up and rubbed her eyes. It was mid-morning, and she had slept in later than usual, exhaustion weighing heavily on her. She had forgotten for a moment where she was until her gaze settled on the room around her. This wasn't her home; it was Sam's, and she remembered she had spent the night here.

Sam had basically put her to bed, and Taylor had fallen into one of the deepest sleeps of her life, her subconscious begging for a respite from the worry, and her body aching from all the nonstop activity surrounding the investigation.

The sound of rustling caught her attention, and Taylor climbed out of bed and went looking for the source.

At the door to Alice's room, her eyes widened in surprise.

Alice was there, hanging a poster on the wall, standing on her tip toes to put it at a height over her head.

"Oh my gosh," Taylor said, covering her mouth in shock.

Alice turned and gave her a huge smile.

"About time you got up, Sleepy Head," she said. "My dad said he even tried to kiss you on the lips an hour ago, and you didn't stir. So much for being his Sleeping Beauty."

Taylor laughed and faintly remembered Sam hovering over her, though she didn't recall the kiss.

"Alice, this is amazing," she said.

In her absence, they had been busy redecorating. The once-plain walls were now adorned with posters and artwork, and the room had transformed into a cozy haven filled with warmth and personality. They'd chosen a theme well, one that couldn't be more fitting for Alice, who gave everyone the impression that she was an old soul.

"Thanks," Alice said proudly. "Me and Dad wanted to get it done before you came back over, as a surprise."

Me and Dad.

That was new, too. Taylor wondered how Sam felt about his new nickname from his daughter.

So much had happened in Taylor's absence, while she was wrapped up in the case, and she felt like she had some catching up to do.

Alice turned back to her poster and began putting sticky putty behind all the corners.

Taylor's gaze wandered around, taking in the delicate touches that spoke of Alice's love for old stories. A vintage map of far-off lands hung proudly above the bed, and a bookshelf on one wall was stocked with classics and tales of adventure. In one corner, a book nook had been created, complete with a wicker chair suspended from the ceiling, an inviting spot to curl up with a good book and escape into another world.

The bed that Sam had brought from his childhood home, that was old wood covered in scars, now looked shiny and white, covered with a very worn but beautiful quilt of yellow and pink blocks. A fuzzy, yellow rug that Taylor had never seen lay across the floor, covering the old hardwoods and serving as a soft landing for late night getting in and out of the bed for the bathroom, or a snack run.

A smile tugged at the corners of Taylor's lips as she noticed the poster Alice was hanging was of Ernest Hemingway, one of her favorite literary personalities. Under the charcoal illustration of him, pencil in hand as he pored over paper on an old-fashioned desk was a quote.

'Today is only one day in all the days that will ever be. But what happens in all the other days that ever come can depend on what you do today.'

Taylor thought about the words for a nanosecond, hoping to find something in them to help her through the heartbreak over Lydia Grimes, but her mind was still too tired to process anything.

"Where is your dad?" Taylor asked. "I want to congratulate him for helping you transform this room." What they had done, to be honest, was create a reflection of Alice's dreams. A perfect sanctuary of imagination and wonder for a young girl who loved to read.

She was so proud of Sam, and a little dismayed that he hadn't needed her help, after all.

"He's outside with Diesel," Alice said, putting up the last

corner and turning to face her. "It took him forever to tempt him away from the bed. He didn't want to leave you. I think he picked up on how upset you are, Taylor. I'm so sorry about your friend's wife."

Taylor couldn't resist the allure of the wicker chair and made her way to the cozy corner. She sat down, letting it twirl gently with her weight until she stopped it with her feet, facing Alice.

"Thank you," she said, when she could speak past the sudden lump in her throat. "It's a sad ending to such a tragic tale. I'm sure you know that they have daughters."

Alice nodded as she went to sit on the bed.

"Three girls who need their mom," Taylor said. "Just like you. Well, a baby and two that are a bit older than you."

"I understand," Alice said somberly. "But it's harder for them. My mom left us by her own choice, but their mom was taken from them. She didn't want to leave her kids."

Taylor saw the pain flash through Alice's face.

"That's true," she said. "Listen, I know you think that your mom didn't want to stay with you and your siblings, but, Alice, sometimes people have too many bad things going on in their heads, making them think false thoughts, like their family would be better off without them. Your mom suffered from a mental illness. Just like some people have cancer—but her sickness was in her brain and affected her feelings and her sense of logic. You know that, right?"

"I do," Alice said. "But it doesn't make me any less angry with her."

"That's okay, too. But, as time passes, I think you'll find that those feelings will change, and I want you to know that it's okay to forgive her. When you are ready, of course."

Alice plucked the throw pillow from her bed, turning it so Taylor could see. She smiled brightly. "Anyway, I hope you like my room."

Taylor returned the smile, genuine warmth washing over her. "I love it, Alice. It's like stepping into a magical world of stories."

Alice beamed with pride, her enthusiasm contagious. "We went to Goodwill, and a bunch of second-hand stores. Dad helped me pick everything out, but he ordered the posters online. He's the best."

Taylor's heart swelled with affection for them both. Despite the trials they had faced recently, they had found a way to bring happiness to their lives. She couldn't be more grateful for the two of them.

Speaking of the recent trials, Taylor wanted to ask Alice a question. She cleared her throat gently. "Alice, how do you feel about the fact that you might not get to see your little brother and sister very often, now that you will be here full time?"

Alice's expression turned thoughtful as she considered the question. "I'll miss them but I'm still glad about the outcome," she said earnestly. "I like living here. I feel wanted. And I know I won't see my little siblings as often, but we can still video chat and stuff. You and Sam will help me keep in touch with them, right?"

Taylor nodded, her heart aching for the young girl's predicament. "Of course. We'll do everything we can to make sure you stay connected with your family. Once they're old enough, maybe they could even come for sleepovers on the weekends."

Alice's eyes sparkled with hope as she continued, "I think the best thing that could happen is that my stepdad, Derek, meets a new woman who will help take care of my little brother and sister. That way, everyone can be happy."

Taylor noticed that Derek had a new name now, too. One he probably would not like at all, but Alice had told them she'd thought of him as a stepparent for years, before it was confirmed.

"That's a nice thought," Taylor said. She couldn't help but admire Alice's resilience and positivity. "Let's pray really hard that a good woman finds him soon."

They heard the door open and the sound of Diesel stampeding through the house, headed their way. Taylor braced herself, ready for him to try to jump in her lap. She heard Sam right behind him and her heart flooded with anticipation.

Sam made everything better for her.

For a minute, Taylor put thoughts of Lydia and her family behind her, and thanked God that she had her own little family to gather round her and show her that, yes, the rains of life would come, but there would always be sunshine to follow.

CHAPTER 30

Cate and Sutton made their way to Luella's modest home, the anticipation weighing heavily on their hearts. Mr. Anderson, the attorney from Jasper, had called them earlier that morning with good news, and they couldn't wait any longer to pass it along.

As they approached the front door, Cate was filled with trepidation mingled with the excitement. They were about to deliver the news that would change Luella's life for the better, but anything could go wrong.

Even though Corbin had covered all the attorney costs involved as well as the security detail he'd put outside her home, he'd decided not to meet Luella. He didn't want to overwhelm her, he said. Sutton remarked later that he was one of a kind, doing what he did without any thought of acknowledgement about it. His talk of balancing the scales was hard to believe. He didn't act like any bully Cate had ever run into.

They knocked gently, and moments later, the door creaked open, revealing the frail but welcoming figure of Luella. Her eyes widened in surprise and delight as she saw Sutton standing on her doorstep.

"Sutton!" Luella exclaimed, her voice trembling with emotion. Tears welled up in her eyes as she reached out to hug her tightly. "Oh, my dear, I've missed you so much. I didn't know if I'd ever see you again."

Sutton returned the embrace, holding Luella close. "I've missed you, too, Luella."

Cate watched the heartfelt reunion, her own eyes misty with emotion. She could see the genuine affection between Sutton and Luella, and it warmed her heart.

"And I'm sorry—what was your name again? Katie?" Luella asked Cate.

"That's close. It's Cate." She leaned in and gave the woman a gentle embrace. "So nice to see you again, Ms. Luella."

After a few moments, they all moved from the foyer into the cozy living room, where they could sit and talk comfortably. The room was large, but cozy with an electric fireplace and colorful rugs and handmade Afghans draping the furniture. Unlike some homes that the elderly lived in alone and couldn't keep up, Luella's was spotless and smelled like something good was cooking. She was also dressed in clean but comfortable-looking clothes. Her hair neatly pinned back and a touch of mascara on her eyelashes. Sutton was right, this wasn't a woman who couldn't take care of herself. Luella Moore was as capable as any of them sitting there.

Cate nodded at Sutton, encouraging her to start.

Sutton took a deep breath. "Luella, I have some wonderful news to share with you. Connor has decided to drop the charges against me for taking the money from your accounts."

Luella's eyes widened in surprise. "He has? That's such a relief. I told him to do it, you know. I must've told him a hundred times that I asked you to take that money and hold it for me. He was angry; he just wouldn't listen."

Sutton smiled, touched by Luella's support. "Yes, Luella, you gave me permission to do it, and that makes all the difference. We have the paperwork right here to show that he's dropped the charges, and another set for you to sign that you did give me the permission to take the money. I brought it with me, too, in a cashier's check, so you can deposit it safely back into your accounts."

Luella looked nervous. "Oh, honey. Are you sure about that? What if he does get into my accounts again and drains everything? Then I'll have no nest egg at all."

"He won't. If he does, he'll be in serious legal trouble. We had this all drawn up by Mr. Anderson, the attorney from Jasper that you met with. It's legal and he signed off. If he gives you one bit of trouble or harassment, we could even slap an order of protection on him, and, believe me, he doesn't want that. It would mess up his spotless record and he'd lose his county commissioner seat."

Luella grimaced. "I don't know about spotless, unless he had it expunged. When he was sixteen, he went to jail for grand larceny. Stole a new Corvette from a lot in Atlanta and took it joyriding for a few days before they caught up with him. He would've rotted in that jail if I hadn't paid for him to have a fancy lawyer. Then I sent his lazy butt to college, and that degree he has on his wall is debt free because of my money. But nothing has ever been enough for Connor. He was a spoiled child who grew into an entitled adult."

"He might feel entitled, but you won't have any more trouble from him. He can go manipulate someone else," Sutton said.

Cate handed over the official documents, and Luella examined them with a mix of relief and gratitude.

"Oh, thank you, dears," she said, her voice quivering. She turned to Sutton again. "I was so worried about you. You've been such a dear friend to me."

Sutton took Luella's hand and squeezed it gently. "I'll always be your friend, Luella. And there's more good news. Connor and Shelly have signed legal documents stating that they no longer wish to pursue guardianship or conservatorship over you."

Luella's eyes filled with tears once again. "You mean I won't have to see them or worry about what they're up to anymore? Oh, Sutton, that's the best news I've heard in a long time."

Sutton nodded, her heart swelling with happiness for her dear friend. "That's right, Luella. You can finally have peace and security."

Cate cleared her throat, wanting to share one more piece of news. "Luella, we also should talk to you about setting up someone you trust as your Power of Attorney when you feel ready."

"What about you, Sutton?" Luella said, clasping Sutton's hands in hers.

"I'm honored by your request, but the attorney believes it's best to appoint someone else, considering all that has happened," Sutton said. "I recall you talking about a niece who is a professor. What about her?"

Luella looked at Sutton with a mix of trust and understanding. "You're right, dear. It would be too much work for you, anyway. You're a busy woman. I'll talk to my niece. But you'll be right alongside me if I need you, won't you?"

Sutton nodded, her eyes shining with sincerity. "Of course, Luella. I'll always be here for you, whatever you need."

Luella smiled; a weight lifted from her shoulders. "I'm so grateful for both of you. Now that this is all settled, I can finally plan that Alaskan cruise with my widow club from church. And I won't have to worry about losing everything and ending up in the funny farm too soon."

They laughed, and Luella asked if they'd like some coffee or tea. Sutton followed her into the kitchen and Cate excused herself briefly.

She slipped outside, and, when she returned, she was cradling a small bundle in her arms. Luella and Sutton were sitting at the kitchen table, a warm casserole dish of lasagna cooling in the middle.

"Would you like some dinner?" Luella asked them.

"No, thank you, but this little guy might," Cate said, then placed the bundle gently on Luella's lap.

A wide-eyed black kitten with soft fur emerged, blinking up at its new owner, and meowed the most pitiful but cutest meow ever.

Luella gasped in surprise, her eyes filling with wonder, and she picked it up and held him to her cheek. "Oh, my goodness! Is this for me?"

Cate nodded, her voice warm with affection. "Yes, Luella, it's for you. This is the same little fellow you've already met. I always keep my promises. There's food, bowls, and litter out on the porch. We've also set up an account at the vet's office with the first year of vaccination and exams all paid for. This little one is yours and he's a rescue, so you're doing a wonderful thing by giving him a safe home."

Luella reached out to stroke the kitten's fur, a radiant smile on her face. "Thank you, Cate. Thank you both. I don't know what I'd do without you."

"The kitten was originally Sutton's idea," Cate said.

Sutton waved her away playfully. "It was both of us. But Luella, what're you going to name him?"

"Oh, goodness. Let's take and warm him in front of the fireplace, and let me think," she said.

They moved to the couch and Luella set the cat on the floor, where he instantly went after a basket that held balls of yarn next to the rocking chair. He did a somersault and landed clumsily on his back feet, looking back at them with surprise.

"He's going to be rowdy," Cate said. "You sure you can handle a kitten?"

Luella nodded emphatically. "I'm sure. It'll be so much fun having his playful energy around. I think I'll name him Soot."

"Cute name," Sutton said.

"Sure is. Other than those white socks, he's black as soot, and it sounds like Sutt. So, I'll think of you fondly every time I call his name," she said, beaming at the cat. "And you, too, Cate," she added.

As they sat together in the cozy living room, surrounded by the warmth of their friendship, Cate knew that they had given Luella something priceless—the gift of a brighter future and the assurance that she would never be alone again.

CHAPTER 31

Cate closed the door to her cottage and walked slowly down the steps and climbed into Taylor's passenger seat. It wasn't often these days that she got to spend alone time with her eldest daughter, and it was sad that Lydia's case would not be closed until they found her remains, but at least they had her killers behind bars. A tiny sliver inside Cate was glad that, for the time being, her daughter could get some rest and family time.

"You look nice," Taylor said.

"Thanks. You do, too. Where're we headed first?"

She'd returned the compliment, but she noticed that Taylor looked like she was still in the jeans and T-shirt that she'd worn around the farm that morning. That was fine, but now she felt out of place.

They pulled out of the driveway and turned right.

Cate pulled at the scarf around her neck, loosening it a bit. She'd gone shopping for something new to wear on her day out with Taylor and, though usually she felt awkward in new clothes, she was glad now that she'd chosen a new pair of well-fitting jeans, cowboy boots, and the soft gray and white scarf. The salesperson had helped her pick it out, saying it looked amazing against her natural gray highlights. She'd found a nice brown leather jacket to top off the outfit and, though it looked expensive, it wasn't.

She'd also taken time to put on makeup, hoping that she looked presentable enough for her daughter to be proud to be seen with her around town.

"Taylor?" Cate said.

"Oh, I'm sorry. Give me one second," she said.

They'd only gone a few hundred yards along the highway and Taylor had the truck barely creeping, like she was looking for something.

"What's wrong? Did a dog get out?" Cate asked, looking out the window worriedly.

"No. Just a minute and I'll explain."

They came to a break in the road where a narrow lane led to a farm gate that straddled a dirt driveway. Cate had seen the newly installed gate a few months before when she was on her way home from rehab but had barely paid attention to it.

Taylor turned in, then stopped in front of the gate. The land behind was a beautiful property of rolling hills with plenty of trees. Cate knew that it was adjacent to the land of their farm, but, as far as she knew, no one lived on it. Taylor had commented once that it included prime lakefront property, just going to waste.

"What's down here?"

"Hold on and I'll show you," Taylor said, then hopped out of the car. She went to the gate and removed the chain that was looped around it and pushed it all the way open before returning to the truck.

She hopped in and put the truck into gear, then slowly moved through the gate.

"Taylor, what is going on?" Cate said, a bit of impatience creeping into her tone. She didn't like to be left in the dark about anything. It came from her past that she always needed to be prepared and know what she was walking into.

"Fine," Taylor said, going around a curve in the long driveway. "We'll stop here."

She stopped the truck again but this time she didn't get out.

"Mom," she said, turning to Cate. "Have I ever asked you to trust me?"

"I—I don't know. Not that I remember, but I do trust you. What's wrong?"

Taylor laughed gently. "Nothing is wrong. Everything is right at this moment. But I want you to trust me and do what I say. If it goes wrong, I'll take full responsibility and I'll spend my life making it up to you, but, for now, I need you to get out of my truck."

Cate pulled her jacket closed, then let it go. Taylor was acting like she'd lost her mind.

"I thought we were going shopping. And for lunch?" she asked her.

"Yeah, we will. Just not today. Go. Please. Take off walking up this driveway and you'll run into what it is that I want you to see. I'll stay right here for the next half an hour, and if, when you get up there, you want me to come pick you up, just call."

"Taylor, is your dad up there? Because I'm sorry, but I do not want to meet with him alone. He's been asking and asking, and it's not going to happen. We're better as friends."

"No, Mom. It's not Dad. Just go—please!"

Cate didn't know what had gotten into Taylor, but she opened her door anyway, then climbed out and started walking. She looked over her shoulder twice, to make sure the truck was still there, but, when she went around yet another curve in the driveway, she could no longer see it.

When she turned back to the road ahead, what she could see stopped her in her tracks.

It was a house nestled into the trees.

Not just any house, but a large, gorgeous log cabin with a wraparound porch complete with white rocking chairs that faced her and the mountains.

In one of those chairs, looking very comfortable, sat Ellis.

Cate almost turned around to head back to the truck and Taylor. But Ellis stood when he saw her and waved. To turn her back on him now would be cruel, so she'd let him say his piece.

Slowly, she walked the rest of the distance to him, and stopped at the foot of the stairs that led to the porch. She craned her neck to look up at the expansive windows framing the second floor or a loft area.

"You look so pretty, Cate," he exclaimed, a huge smile breaking on his face. "Come on up and look at the view from here."

She climbed the steps, feeling heavier with each one.

He didn't try to touch her when she got there. He knew from her body language that she wouldn't be receptive. But he stood close, staring down into her eyes.

She could smell the woodsy, clean scent of him. Months ago, she would've melted into his arms, glad to feel the sense of security that he brought her. He didn't look any different. Or, at least, any worse for wear. If anything, he looked healthier, his face tan and lined, his muscles just about popping through his shirt sleeves.

"Ellis, why am I here? Why are you here? Whose house is this?"

Suddenly, before she could react, he sunk to one knee and pulled a box from his pocket.

"It's our house, if you'll allow it, Cate. And I want you to live in it with me. Will you marry me?"

Cate's eyes were so wide she could feel the breeze on her cornea. Her pulse was pounding in her ears, and she trembled.

"What are you doing?" she finally squeaked out.

He laughed. "I'm proposing, woman. And my knee is killing me, so I wish you'd go ahead and answer."

"But Ellis—you ... I ..."

"None of that matters. Whatever it is you're going to say, Cate, don't. What matters is that I know you love me. You can't make me believe you don't. And there's no doubt in this world that I love you. I bought the property next to the farm and I've spent the last eight months building this place as a surprise to you. The fact that you shut me out along the way hurt me, but I kept going, knowing I could win you back."

"Ellis, you know I don't care anything about material things," she said. "The house is beautiful and all, but—"

He held his hand up to stop her from talking.

"Yes, I do know that. I also know that you would never go with me to Atlanta, or any place that is not near your girls, or the farm. We have fifty acres here, Cate. I've even cut a trail straight through to the farm, where you can get to work easily. We can expand your business, the rescue, and really build a legacy. You and I together. All of us."

Her mind was reeling. Cate couldn't believe that he'd been right next to her all these months, building this amazing house. And she'd thought he was going on with his life without her.

"What do your kids think about this?" she asked.

He shifted to the other knee, grunting in pain, but she had to give it to him, he wouldn't get up. He kept holding the ring box, and she tried not to look at the sparkle coming off the diamond. He looked so uncomfortable.

She was starting to feel sorry for him.

"They're happy that I'll be happy. So much so that my daughter has been out here supervising the kitchen layout, the painters, and all the other little details that need a woman's touch. But, if they weren't happy, I wouldn't care. I don't need their blessing, Cate. All I need is you. Since you came into my life, I have hope for the future. Hope to do something meaningful. I thought that I'd lost that years ago and even my kids can see that you make me a better man."

"Would you please stand up, Ellis?" She said when he moaned.

"No, I won't. Not until you answer my question. I'll stay here until I turn into a petrified old man who falls over and rots into the boards of this porch. One day they'll find me and write a fairytale about me—the old man whose heartache turned him to petrified wood."

Cate tried to muffle a laugh.

"Why didn't you just come out and tell me about this when you told me you were selling the boat?" she asked.

He looked instantly somber.

"Maybe it was a mistake, but let me ask you a question; when in your lifetime has someone ever given you a wonderful surprise?"

She hesitated.

"Never, that I can remember," she said finally.

He nodded. "Exactly. But you deserve it more than anyone I've ever met! You are smart, beautiful, and the kindest soul. You do everything for everyone else, never asking anything in return. So, forgive me if for once in your life I wanted to really blow your mind with a big gesture of love. To surprise you and let you know that you are worth this." He held his arms out wide, and nearly lost his balance. "All this. You're worth every acre. Every board and nail, and every decision that drove me nuts on materials. And you're worth even more than all that. I never thought I would love again, and you gave that back to me, Cate. You've made my life worth living again when, *for* so long, it wasn't. Don't you understand what you mean to me?"

When he finished his speech, he wasn't the only one with tears in his eyes.

They were now running down Cate's face.

"But I guess I was wrong," he said sadly. "I thought you felt the same and that you would be happy at starting over."

Cate's heart ached for the sadness she saw on his face. She'd been so stubborn. And so very stupid.

He started to get up and she pushed his shoulder down.

"Wait," she said softly.

"Wait?"

"Yes."

"Yes? Do you mean yes, wait, or yes-yes?" he looked earnest, his eyes full of hope.

"Yes, yes," she whispered, even though the words filled her with fear of the unknown. She still couldn't quite believe that someone like Ellis would ever be able to love someone like her. It didn't make sense. Things like this just didn't happen to people like her.

He jumped to his feet and slid the ring on her shaking finger, then grabbed her up in his arms and swung her around as he yodeled into the air like a maniac.

Laughter spilled from Cate, from the very depths of her soul like she never remembered it doing before, and she begged him to put her down. He acted like she weighed nothing, and it made her feel like a girl again.

"I'm dizzy," she called out, slapping his back playfully.

Finally, he stopped and took her to a rocking chair and gently set her down. He lowered himself into the chair next to her and took her hand, looking at the ring on her finger.

"We're going to be married," he said breathlessly, grinning like a possum.

"Yep, seems so," Cate replied, her cheeks warm. She envisioned herself in a wedding dress, in front of a preacher, maybe even in a tiny church.

Just a small gathering. Nothing fancy.

A country wedding like she'd always dreamed of but never had the opportunity to do.

"Oh, hold on," she said. "We're still waiting on Sam and Taylor to set a date. I don't want to upstage them. Can we keep our engagement a secret for a while?"

"On one condition," Ellis said. "I'll wait as long as you want for everyone else to know we're engaged, but you have to move in with me right this minute. The house is ready. All you have to do is bring Brandy, put your clothes in the closet, and your finishing touch on the decorations. I won't stay here without you, Cate. I helped build every square foot of this house, keeping thoughts of you in mind with every decision it took to finish it. If you won't live in it, I'll sell it tomorrow and never look back."

Cate stood and went to the porch railing. She looked at the view from the porch. She could see the Blue Ridge mountains, and the sun beginning to set over them. She knew that somewhere in the backyard of this house, it overlooked the lake. Ellis knew that water was the one thing that brought her the most peace. He would've taken advantage of the view and she would bet that whatever he'd built to see it from, it was astounding.

If she'd ever dared to dream of her own home, it would've looked just like this one. Not something gigantic or fancy that people would ooh and aah over and be envious of. Just a simple home nestled within the woods as though it were always a part of the landscape, inviting the magic of nature inside to rub elbows and live with them, filling them with love and contentment.

Ellis came up behind her and put his arms around her. She could feel his solidness. His warmth, and, yes, his love.

"This house wasn't built for me, Ellis," she said.

She felt his body stiffen behind her.

"It was built for *us*," she finished, then felt him lean into her, taking every bit of her body within the curve of his, as he finally felt that he'd done what he set out to do. Ellis had brought the love of his life home, where she belonged.

CHAPTER 32

Having Thanksgiving the first week of December felt strange, but hopefully next year would be different. The rain had finally gone, and the weather was unusually warm, sunshine bright in the sky and beaming down on the farm. Taylor hoped it would dry out all the mud and puddles quickly, so they wouldn't have such a hard time keeping the animals clean. She was back to doing her share of the chores, and she didn't mind getting down and dirty, minus the wet mud.

Anna's house smelled divine, and everyone looked so happy, but it was a bittersweet time for Taylor. She tried to keep her mind off the Grimes family tragedy and keep a smile on her face for everyone else, especially Sam and Alice who, now that the paternity and custody question was official, were going through a new phase of awkwardness. It was no longer just a possibly temporary set up. They were going to be together until Alice went off to college, or whatever she did to step into adulthood.

Even though Sam had taken the lead in making Alice comfortable in his home, he was depending on Taylor to help ease the way into getting into a family routine where they could feel normal.

Taylor told him he needed to relax, and then things would fall into place on their own, but he was still struggling with the question of whether he could be a good dad or not.

Speaking of dads, Samuel Sr. was joining them for the first time, and Taylor couldn't get over how much Sam looked and talked like him. Like Sam, his dad was a friendly guy, with lots of good stories to keep conversation going. He was also making a special effort to treat Alice like a granddaughter, and Taylor had seen him initiating interaction with her several times already.

"Here comes the turkey," Anna called out from the kitchen.

She led the way and Cecil carried the huge platter, then set it on the table. Anna handed him the carving tools, but he hesitated.

"If you all don't mind," he said, "I'd like to say a prayer."

Taylor glanced at her dad, who had taken the head of the table on one end. No one told him to, but, also, no one had the guts to tell him not to. Though he hadn't yet earned their respect, they would still give it to him. At least he was still sober, and that deserved its own celebration.

Cecil bowed his head and the silence spread through the kitchen, then the living room where the kids' table was set up.

"Dear Heavenly Father, as we gather 'round this Southern table, with thankful hearts as big as a stable, we lift our voices in gratitude today, for all the blessings you've sent our way.

We thank you for the food we share, for the love and kindness that's in the air, for family and friends, near and far, for the warmth of this home, like a guiding star. We ask for your continued grace, as we navigate life's daily race, And please, Lord, if it's not too much, help us resist that extra piece of pecan pie with a gentle touch. In your name, we pray, Amen!"

"Amen," everyone said, and Cecil began carving.

He would sit at the other end of the table, a spot he was invited to take. After the last year of him spending so much time living at the farm part-time and elbows deep in every project he could take on, her sisters and Cate were nearly as fond of him as

Taylor was, and he'd become the unofficial patriarch of the family. The kids adored him, and that made her heart happy that he felt like he had a family in them.

Her dad would just have to accept that, if he wanted to continue to play a big part in their lives. Thankfully, he hadn't brought a girlfriend with him, but, on the other hand, that might be another indication that he was not going to give up trying to win Cate back.

That train had left the station. Ellis sat beside Cate, and he'd barely taken his eyes off her all day. They were together again, and the waves of contentment that came off them were palpable. It made Taylor happy to see her mother smiling again, but it did bring her a bit of sadness for her dad.

He had to witness all the rest of them doing so well, with relationships as well as their boarding business, and even the rescue. But he was still floundering, still living in the same shoddy trailer, alone most nights, for all Taylor knew.

Still doing his best to stay sober.

She wondered if he looked at Anna's house and regretted losing it.

Well, technically, it was still Taylor's house. She had to admit, if only to herself, she missed it. Her cottage was nice, and it had a wonderful view of the lake, but she and this house went way back. She'd scrambled to grab it from the auction and struggled to keep it for years until she'd gotten her finances going steady. There were days that she wished she hadn't offered Anna to live in it, but her sister and the kids needed it, and Taylor would never take it back.

She just hoped that Anna cared about it as much as Taylor did.

On that note, Taylor had half expected Anna to have a date for today, but no, her sister was keeping her cards close to the vest in the relationship department. At least she wasn't the only one flying solo. Of course, dating was not on Jo's mind at all, but

Shane hadn't shown up for Lucy, either. He was with his parents, her little sister had said, and she didn't seem bothered by it. It was strange to Taylor that he never mentioned his mom and dad to her, but today he'd skipped the Gray Thanksgiving for them. Maybe her wish had come true and the flames between Shane and Lucy were fizzling out.

Beneath the table, Sam reached over and squeezed her hand. He was probably reading her mind again, something he seemed to have a knack for, and he knew how nervous she was to have everyone in the same room at the same time.

Or he was sympathizing with her about Lydia Grimes. Somewhere out there, Lydia's body rested uncomfortably, longing for a proper burial. Taylor didn't know how Caleb and the girls would ever be able to go on, especially not having Lydia's remains, but she hoped, for their sake, time would help heal.

"I think that's enough turkey carved," Cecil said, then took his seat.

Jo had outdone herself with the table, putting together a rustic centerpiece of gourds and pinecones, flanked with an assortment of plates in deep autumn colors. She'd done the same for the kids' table, and it felt like they were at a fancy restaurant. Crazy thing was that Jo had found everything she needed, including the plates and glasses, at secondhand stores, with some embellishments from the Dollar General, but no one would ever guess it.

Her work rivaled some of the fanciest table designs Taylor had ever seen photographs of in magazines.

They began passing each dish around, heaping their plates with turkey, green bean casserole, and sweet potato pie, among other dishes. They had enough food to feed an army and, now, Taylor was glad that Cate had invited Corbin, Sutton, and her two daughters.

Sutton's girls were twins, though it was obvious that other than in looks, they were completely different. Both were exceptionally smart and had obviously been taught impeccable manners. And, like their mother, they both seemed smitten with Corbin.

Taylor had already seen them grab at least a dozen selfies with him to post on their Instagram.

Corbin was taking it well, but she'd spotted Sutton pull the girls into the pantry a few minutes before they'd sat down to eat, to put a stop to the fanfare. She'd hissed at them to just treat him like everyone else, not like a celebrity.

Taylor wondered just where that was going with him and Sutton, but it wasn't her business, so she would just have to watch it play out. The sheriff had taken her aside and told her the charges on Sutton were dropped, and that Cate had something to do with it.

Whatever had happened, Taylor was happy for Sutton, and it was nice to have the sheriff's gratitude in her pocket. Once everyone went home, she planned to talk to Cate about the details.

"Thank you, ladies, for your help today," Anna said. "Couldn't have pulled it off without my sisters, and you, Mom."

"I doubt that," Lucy joked, and they all laughed.

She was right, too. Anna didn't need them for help in the kitchen, but they'd had fun cooking together, laughing, and building a great memory with Cate among them. It was like a scene that Taylor had dreamed of many times as a teenager, when she herself tried to piece together their holiday meals, from whatever she could get her hands on or find in the pantry.

She shoveled a huge bit of mashed potatoes and gravy into her mouth and closed her eyes in delight. They could take every dish off the table, except for the potatoes and gravy, and she'd still be happy. She wasn't a sweet potato kind of girl, but she was glad to see that Sutton's sweet potato casserole was getting demolished, too.

Taylor stole a glance at Jo, who looked to be doing her best to stay positive for the day. Eldon had been right there with them at the table for their last big family meal and Taylor was sure that this was a brutal event for Jo to get through, and she sent her some silent, positive vibes. Jo had told her earlier that morning that she'd decided to go ahead and talk to a therapist, that the guilt and shame for bringing Eldon in among them, and nearly taking Cate's life, was more than she could manage on her own.

Taylor was thrilled that Jo was going to seek help. For her sake and Levi's. Maybe she'd get him to someone, too.

Laughter broke out in the living room and Taylor looked to see Johnny digging into his plate with both hands, the older kids egging him on with attention.

Levi laughed the loudest and it did Taylor's heart good to hear him. He was a kid who needed his cousins around him. They brought out the side of him that could laugh and put his troubles aside for a moment.

Lucy jumped up from her chair, darting in there with a napkin to clean Johnny up before he touched any of Anna's furniture. She scolded him, without much force, and told him if he did it again, he wouldn't get dessert. She was such a good mother. And now, much more than that. A career woman with lots of opportunities on the horizon. Someone had picked up the story about the showing she'd put together for Faire's art, and Lucy had jumped on it and set up social media platforms for Faire, highlighting some of her best pieces.

Lucy had a talent for the social media, and one of her reels had gone viral, and, suddenly, Faire's work was in demand. She'd sold a lot of it, for prices that no one—especially Faire—would've dreamed of. Lucy was now filtering through requests from struggling artists, asking her to represent them or help them get their art discovered.

For now, Lucy was taking her commissions and putting them in a savings account, for if she ever got down on her luck again, she said.

Taylor had a feeling that Lucy's down and out days were over. She was so proud of her, and it appeared that her rebellious little sister had finally grown up, and out of the urge to leave havoc behind in every path she walked.

"Who wants dessert?" Anna called out, and the kids came running.

Taylor went to help, and she scooped ice cream over the pie that Anna dished onto a paper plate, then handed it to each kid. All but Levi, their country boy who insisted on banana pudding, saying it was un-American not to eat the pudding for Thanksgiving.

One by one, including Wyn leading Johnny by the hand, they disappeared out the door, taking their plates with them to go play with the litter of puppies.

Suddenly the house was peacefully soundless, except for Anna who still puttered around in the kitchen.

"Okay, everyone," she said, finally coming to stand at the head of the table. "Now that the kids are outside, I have an announcement before you get your dessert."

Sam booed at her playfully, but they all quieted, giving her the floor.

"As you all know, it's been a long legal battle to get anything from Pete for my divorce settlement, and me and the kids have struggled but we've made do. Not only did Pete claim to have lost most of our money through bad investments and gambling, but he was also being sued. That led to a forensic accountant being hired by the attorney's office and, turns out, Pete wasn't completely broke."

Taylor watched Anna's face transform.

"They found enough that, after his restitution is paid, I'll be awarded the rest. It's a substantial amount. At least enough that the kids and I are going to be okay!"

"That's wonderful, Anna," Cate said, her expression one of relief.

"I agree," Jackson said. "Good for you. And I hope that piece of crap husband of yours gets what he's got coming."

"I agree, Dad. Just don't talk like that in front of the kids," Anna scolded. "He's still their father."

Jackson continued to grumble under his breath about Pete.

Taylor had a feeling that Pete would get every piece of black destiny due to him. He'd already been found guilty of a lot of bad things, and his sentencing was coming up. It was tough for the kids to have a father in prison, but it wasn't like they were going to be missing anything. Pete had basically dumped them when he and Anna split up. The kids didn't even ask about him anymore, though she knew that could change as they matured.

"Hallelujah," Lucy said. "But Anna, I hope this doesn't mean you're going back to your old ways. We kind of like the new Anna who isn't afraid to step out of the house without being dressed to the nines or having every hair in place. The new you is much easier to deal with."

Anna laughed, another monumental moment. A comment like that from Lucy in the past would've started a war. Taylor felt a rush of pride. It seemed the Gray sisters were truly growing up and learning how to get along.

"Nope—I've learned my lesson. No designer clothes or bags. I'll keep the same car, until the wheels fall off, too. I'll be very careful with every penny, but I do have some plans I'm exploring. More on that after I've done all the research," Anna said. "But I don't want to tarnish today by spiraling into anything negative, so let's talk about something else."

The door opened and Alice came in, the rest of the kids trailing behind her.

"That was fast," Taylor said.

"Johnny has to pee," Levi said. "I'll take him."

"I have an announcement, too," Sam said, then stood so everyone could hear him.

Levi whispered to Johnny to hold on a second, that he wanted to hear.

Taylor looked at Alice, who was beaming from where she had taken a chair next to her new grandpa, Samuel. She knew that everyone would be told about her new status today.

Sam gestured toward Alice. "I want you all to know that it's now official, Alice—my daughter as proved by science—will be living with us permanently and will soon, after the process is complete, be known as Alice Elizabeth Stone."

Everyone applauded, and Alice blushed, but you could see the joy pouring off her.

Taylor caught Cate's glance. Her mother nodded at her approvingly, knowing it was a big deal for her, too. Taylor would be a full time stepmom, and that was sure to change the dynamic of her life.

"And that's all," Sam said, "unless someone else wants to take the floor with more life-changing news."

"I've met someone," Corbin called out, then turned to stare straight at Sutton, who instantly turned red. "I might write her a love song."

She slapped at him playfully.

They all laughed and smaller conversations broke out again.

Sam elbowed Taylor, nodding at his dad who had begun telling Corbin about the time he met Alan Jackson after the tour bus broke down in Sam's hometown and they called his shop to come fix it. He had them all laughing about a young Sam standing outside the bus door, singing a Jackson tune at the top of his lungs, hoping to get discovered and added to the band.

"He's got stories, doesn't he?" Sam joked to Taylor. "Hope he doesn't ask me to sing it for them."

"I love it. I'm going to pick his brain for everything he can tell me to embarrass you."

"Go right ahead," Sam whispered, leaning in toward Taylor.

"By the way, since it's the day to be vocal about it, I just want you to know that I'm thankful for you."

"I'm thankful for you, too, Sam."

He grabbed her hand again under the table. "No, I mean it. You are the absolutely, positively best thing that has ever happened to me, and I'll spend the rest of my life thanking my lucky stars that I went through the pain of losing my dog, because it led me to you. It was worth every excruciating day that I kicked myself with guilt over giving Diesel up. Not only did I get him back, but I got you as the grand prize. I am a lucky man, Taylor."

She didn't know what to say. He had a better way with words than she did. No one had ever talked to her like that. No one had ever loved her so deeply. So thoroughly.

"I feel the same way, Sam," she said, knowing her response was lame, but not knowing what else to say.

He chuckled. "You have such a way with words. I bet you're great at poetry."

She punched his arm playfully "Shut up. You know what I mean."

"Of course I do," he said, his tone turning teasing as he sang quietly in her ear. *"You love me. You want to kiss me. You want to keep me and do naughty things to me."*

Taylor blushed, the heat crawling up her neck and into her face.

"Okay, I'll stop," Sam said, laughing. "I just have one more thing to say and then I'll leave you alone and I'll go get us some pecan pie."

"What?"

"I know that today is about the whole family and not just us, but, before the sun sets tonight, I want to have a date confirmed."

"A date? Like for —" her heart began pounding out of her chest. Was he really going to put her on the spot? A specific date would make it so real. A countdown would start and begin ticking in her ears.

"—Yep. For our wedding," he interrupted. "I want Alice to have a home with two parents. One where we do things right. And even if we didn't have her to push it along, I'm ready to call you my wife, Taylor."

He looked so earnest. So sweet and honest.

She couldn't let him down.

"When were you thinking?" she asked quietly, so that no one else would hear. "Next year sometime? Year after next?"

"Nope," he said, shaking his head. "I'm thinking this month. A Christmas wedding, right here on the farm or in a church in town. Whatever you want. Something simple that doesn't take a lot of preparation, yet something memorable. Alice and I will plan it and, if you want, all you have to do is show up."

Taylor felt light-headed. Christmas was barely three weeks away.

It felt sudden.

And terrifying.

But in her heart, buried deep under all her issues of feeling unloved, abandoned, and not worthy, she knew that Christmas would be the perfect time. Having Sam as her husband would be the single best present she'd ever received.

"I'm thinking December twenty-sixth would be perfect," Sam said softly. "You'll be a beautiful winter bride."

"Okay," she whispered, feeling astonished that she was able to utter a single word. But, when it was out, it suddenly felt so right, and something shifted within her.

This was long overdue, and she knew, it was time. *Her* time.

The End (Keep Turning the page for a surprise!)

HELLO READERS! I hope you enjoyed book eight in the *Hart's Ridge* series. If you'd like to know more about where the mystery plot for this book, Starting Over, came from, keep flipping pages until you get to the FROM THE AUTHOR section. There you will find the backstory for the true crime inspiration in the mystery plot of this story.

Oh, Surprise! Originally, *Hart's Ridge* was going to be only eight books. Because of the huge popularity and the ongoing love of the Gray family, you can now order book nine in the *Hart's Ridge* series here: [Blackbird] Would you like a sneak peek? I've added the first chapter below for your enjoyment:

Blackbird: Chapter One

Life was strange. One day you're going along, and everything is fine—or at least your definition of fine at the time, minus the usual challenges that just being human throws at you—and then suddenly it's upside down and your only thought is of surviving, minute by minute.

For the woman trapped in the confines of a dark and dingy room in a madman's basement, life had become a delicate balance between hope and despair. Every day, as the first rays of sunlight filtered through the tiny window high above, she would wake up and remind herself to stay busy. It was the only way to keep her from slipping into the depths of despair. To push away the dread of a visit from him.

Domnus.

The name meant master; he'd told her.

Her response was a blank stare.

It infuriated him.

But she did have one friend. A finely feathered one, at that.

She lived for the visits from Blackbird. He'd heard her move with the chain from the other side of the window and he came to comfort her. Nearly every day now.

At the close of their visits, he'd lift his head and raise his wings a bit, then call out loudly as he looked around.

Conk-la-ree, conk-la-ree ...

It looked and felt like he was trying to tell someone she was there, to come rescue and release her from her concrete prison. The woman often found solace in the melodious songs he sang, as if the blackbird was an embodiment of her longing for freedom. But, as much as she wanted to reach out and touch him, their connection remained intangible, restricted by the invisible barriers that separated them.

She had no idea exactly how long she'd been there. On occasion, she was drugged and, when she awoke, she felt it could've been hours or days.

It wasn't more than a handful of months, she felt sure of that. Her hair was long. On her head and her body, but then it had always grown fast.

She had learned to live in the present, to focus on the tasks that kept her occupied within the confines of her room. Pushing away thoughts of home and staying busy became her means of survival, a way to drown out the eerie silence that pervaded the space around her.

She had crafted her own routine, finding purpose in the simplest of activities. Each morning, she meticulously made her bed, smoothing the wrinkled sheet and fluffing the faded pillow that graced the soiled mattress in the corner.

It was a small act, but it gave her a sense of order in the chaos of her situation.

Then, she would set about cleaning her meager surroundings. With a makeshift broom fashioned from discarded clothes and a broken handle, she would sweep away the dust and debris that had accumulated since her last cleaning session. It was a never-ending battle against the grit and grime, but it gave her a semblance of control over her environment.

Afterward, she sat by the small, barred window, watching as the outside world moved on without her. Nothing much happened on the ground. A random squirrel. A dog walking by.

But the sky always changed.

The sky was her canvas. The clouds her paint and the tool that allowed her imagination to take flight. She would discover stories in their makeup, imagining what it would be like to be part of that vibrant tapestry. In those stolen moments of reverie, she would lose herself.

Time became her enemy and her ally, as the days blended into one another. She marked the passage of time with the growth of the morning glory vine she'd found behind the discarded wardrobe cabinet. It had found a way in through a crack at the foundation, dipping in from the ground level and then raising its head inside.

She tended it with care and watched it thrive under her nurturing touch. It reminded her of the resilience of life, and she drew strength from its steady growth.

As each day would draw to a close, the music would start, and he would come.

She'd resisted at first, but he'd broken her spirit after he'd broken bones. A nose that would never be straight again. A wrist that had healed awkwardly.

Pain was a mighty convincer.

The will to live wasn't easily squashed.

Especially when she had children waiting for her to find her way home.

The music became her refuge, a way to escape what he was doing to her body. She would close her eyes and let the notes carry her away, imagining herself dancing freely in an ethereal realm beyond the prison walls.

And so, she danced. In the dimly-lit room, the stench of his scent threatening to suffocate her, she twirled and swayed, her movements graceful and fluid, as if she were performing on a grand stage. With closed eyes, she envisioned herself surrounded by an audience, their applause echoing in her ears, a reminder that she was more than just a prisoner.

In those moments, she could transcend the confines of her physical space and the abuse. In her mind, the room transformed into a vast ballroom, adorned with sparkling chandeliers and ornate decorations. She was no longer a captive, but a radiant performer, captivating the hearts of those who watched her with awe.

Sometimes, she would choreograph intricate routines, mapping out the steps in her mind as she danced. Each movement became a rebellion against her captivity, a declaration of her indomitable spirit. She would leap and spin, her body a vessel of expression, defying the limitations imposed upon her.

As the music swelled within her, her heart soared, and, for a moment, she could forget the bleakness of her reality. In the realm of her imagination, she was free—free to express herself, free to dream, and free to hope.

But, inevitably, he would finish, and the music would fade. The applause would cease, and she would find herself alone in the darkness once again. The room would revert to its oppressive reality, and the weight of her confinement would settle upon her shoulders.

The guilt and horror of what he'd done to her was always left in his wake.

Yet, despite the crushing despair that threatened to engulf her, she clung to the fragments of joy she found within her daily activities. She knew that was not just a means of distraction, but a lifeline that kept her spirit alive. It was her way of asserting her humanity, refusing to be reduced to a mere captive.

And so, she would continue to rise each day. Continue to make her bed, clean her surroundings. She would continue to lose herself in the simplicity of a bird, a plant, and the swatch of sky she could see from her window. She would mark each day with purpose, carving out moments of solace and defiance within the bleakness of her existence.

As long as she could stay busy, as long as she could hold onto the fragments of her true self, she believed that there was still hope. Hope for rescue, hope for freedom, and hope for a future where the songs of the blackbird would be joined by her own voice, lifted in triumphant harmony as she was reunited with her children.

And, in the depths of her captivity, she always remembered to whisper to the departing blackbird with unwavering determination, "Thank you for not forgetting about me."

To read more of Blackbird, book nine in the *Hart's Ridge* series, follow the link [here].

FROM THE AUTHOR

Hello, readers! I hope you enjoyed Starting Over, the eighth book in the *Hart's Ridge* series. The true crime wrapped into the fictional town of Hart's Ridge and its fictional characters was loosely inspired by the carjacking and abduction of Alice Donovan.

Chadrick Evans Fulks, of West Hamlin, W.Va., and Brandon Basham were sentenced to death for kidnapping and killing 44-year-old Alice Donovan of Galivants Ferry, S.C., in December 2002. Donovan disappeared from a Walmart parking lot in Conway, S.C. Her remains were not found until 2009. The case of Serenity Bond was loosely inspired from the same crime spree by Fulks and Basham in which they also abducted a young college student named Samantha Burns, who was never seen again. Her body has not been recovered as of the time of this publication.

My deepest condolences to the Donovan and Burns family, as well as other people who were victims of the Fulks and Basham crime spree.

If you've enjoyed the eight books of Hart's Ridge, you'll be happy to know that I've decided to continue the series and I'm

FROM THE AUTHOR

working on the next book now. In the meantime, I invite you to join my private Facebook group, Kay's Krew, where you can be part of my focus group, giving ideas for story details such as names, livelihoods, etc. to this series. I'm also known to entertain with stories of my life with the Bratt Pack and all the kerfuffle's I find myself getting into. Please join my author newsletter to hear of future Hart's Ridge books, as well as giveaways and discounts.

Until then,

Scatter kindness everywhere.

Kay Bratt

AUTHOR BIO

PHOTO © 2021 STEPHANIE CRUMP
PHOTOGRAPHY

Writer, Rescuer, Wanderer

Kay Bratt is the powerhouse author behind over 30 internationally bestselling books that span genres from mystery and women's fiction to memoir and historical fiction. Her books are renowned for delivering an emotional wallop wrapped in gripping storylines. Her Hart's Ridge small-town mystery series earned her the coveted title of Amazon All Star Author and continues to be one of her most successful projects out of her more than million books sold around the world.

Kay's literary works have sparked lively book club discussions wide-reaching, with her works translated into multiple languages, including German, Korean, Chinese, Hungarian, Czech, and Estonian.

Beyond her writing, Kay passionately dedicates herself to rescue missions, championing animal welfare as the former Director of Advocacy for Yorkie Rescue of the Carolinas. She considers herself a lifelong advocate for children, having volunteered extensively in a Chinese orphanage and supported nonprofit organizations like An Orphan's Wish (AOW), Pearl River Outreach, and Love Without Boundaries. In the USA, Kay served as a Court Appointed Special Advocate (CASA) for abused and neglected children in Georgia, as well as spearheaded numerous outreach programs for underprivileged kids in South Carolina.

As a wanderlust-driven soul, Kay has called nearly three dozen different homes on two continents her own. Her globetrotting adventures have taken her to captivating destinations across Mexico, Thailand, Malaysia, China, the Philippines, Central America, the Bahamas, and Australia. Today, she and her soulmate of 30 years find their sanctuary by the serene banks of Lake Hartwell in Georgia, USA.

Described as southern, spicy, and a touch sassy, Kay loves to share her life's antics with the Bratt Pack on social media. Follow her on Facebook, Twitter, and Instagram to join the fun.

For more information, visit www.kaybratt.com.